Index

The term Deco has many interpretations. A Deco can range from a simple paper book with pictures and clippings to elaborate combinations of stunning artwork. Themes for a deco are unlimited. For instance, our designers made decos about becoming a grandmother, women they admire, traveling in foreign lands, and gardening. They even drew inspiration from the items found in their purses. Decos can contain any array of artwork - paper art, photography, stamping, stitching, beadwork. As you can see, a deco can be any style, theme, or shape you want it to be.

A Deco can be made by just one person, but you may choose to create one in a group, round-robin style. If you are going to organize a swap, please keep the following in mind: a) ability level and output quality should be consistent among members of the group; b) the deco must be a size that can be mailed in a standard size padded manila envelope; c) each artist must sign their work; d) everyone must know and follow the rules for completion of the projects.

One of the wonderful things about swapping these miniature works of art is that one day, your Deco is returned to you filled with artwork from several artists.

An Altered Deco is inspiring.
A Deco is a treasure.
Your Deco is a true keepsake.

Faux Star Ancestor Book
Pages 8 - 11

Angel Board Book
Pages 12 - 15

CD Deco Book
Pages 16 - 21

Vintage Greetings Book
Pages 22 - 25

Wonderful Women Book
Pages 26 - 29

I'm a Grandma Book
Pages 30 - 33

In the Garden Book
Pages 34 - 39

Memories in My Purse Book
Pages 40 - 43

The Eyes Have It Book
Pages 44 - 47

Ooh - la - la! Paris! Book
Pages 48 -51

1. Trace lid onto cardboard, Black paper and background paper.

2. Glue paper to cardboard.

3. Punch holes in paper and cardboard, glue all layers together.

4. Place BBs, glue lid to paper.

Binding the Book Signatures

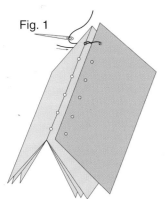

Fig. 1

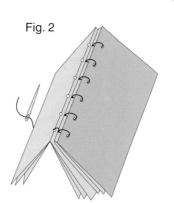

Fig. 2

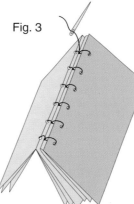

Fig. 3

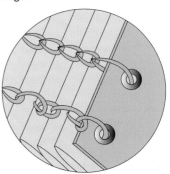

Fig. 4

Let's Play... Games Book

*an original design
by Keely Barham*

MATERIALS:

Design Originals Legacy Collage Papers (#0538 Peter's Dream, #0542 Father's Farm, #0544 Bingo, #0554 Diamonds, #0555 Tags, #0497 TeaDye Letters, #0527 Pink Diamonds, #0551 Legacy Words, #0411 Letter Postcards) • Two 4" x 7" pieces of heavy-duty chipboard • 30 pieces of 7" x 7 1/2" text weight paper • Black cardstock • Thin cardboard • 2" diameter glass-topped tin container (*Coffee Break Designs*) • Five 4.5mm steel BBs • Twelve 1/8" Extra long eyelets & eyelet setter • Miscellaneous game pieces & ephemera • Black waxed linen thread • Elastic cording • Bone folder • Japanese screw punch • Awl • Glue stick • Quicktite Super Glue Gel • E6000

How to Make the Book

INSTRUCTIONS:

Cover both pieces of the heavy-duty chipboard, front and back, with papers. Mark placement for eyelets on the spine side of each covered board 1/4" from edge and at 1" intervals. Punch holes with Japanese screw punch. Set the eyelets in holes. For the tilt game, remove glass lid from tin container (set aside base for another use) and place over scrap of Bingo paper. Trace with a pencil and cut out. Trace lid on scrap of thin cardboard, cut out and glue with glue stick to back of Bingo paper. Punch 5 random holes. Trace lid on scrap of Black cardstock, cut and glue to back of cardboard. Glue this to front cover. Put one BB in each hole of tilt game. Put a small amount of Super glue on the rim of the glass lid. Place over tilt game. Note: Do not move cover until glue is set. Glue letter tiles to front cover with E6000, set aside to dry. Using the bone folder, fold all of the text paper so that the folded sheet measures 3 3/4" x 7". Arrange the folded sheets into 6 signatures of 5 sheets each. Cut 6 pieces of collage papers to 7" x 7 1/2". Fold each sheet as above and cover each signature with a different collage paper. With the awl, drill binding holes in the fold of each signature at 1" intervals.

CHAIN STITCH BINDING:

Cut a 2-yard length of waxed linen and thread an embroidery needle. Start sewing from the inside of the first signature. Sew out the top hole and leave an 8" tail. Sew through the top hole of the front cover from the inside to the outside and then back into the top hole of the first signature. Tie the ends together in a knot and trim off the excess tail. (Fig. 1) Sew out the second hole; sew through the second hole in the front cover and back into the signature. Repeat until you have come to the last hole. Instead of going back into the first signature, add another signature. With the needle make a half hitch knot around the thread coming from the last hole and then sew down into the last hole of the second (new) signature. (Fig. 2) Sew out the next hole. With your needle, go under the previous stitch and back into the signature. This makes the chain stitch. (Fig. 3) Repeat in this way making chain stitches and adding new signatures until all of the signatures have been bound. (Fig. 4) Note: Make sure that when you add a new signature that the paper is facing the correct way. Add the back cover by sewing from the inside to the outside of the hole and then back into the last signature. The last signature will have two rows of stitching on the inside. Tie off inside the last signature using half hitch knots.

Create your own book with Legacy Collage papers from Beth Cote. These lovely papers combine perfectly with old game pieces, found objects and ephemera. Use this fabulous book to journal and sketch. Saving your precious memories and thoughts is inspiring and important.

Inside Front Cover and Beginning of Signature One

Let's Play... Games Book

End of Signature One and Beginning of Signature Two

End of Signature Two and Beginning of Signature Three

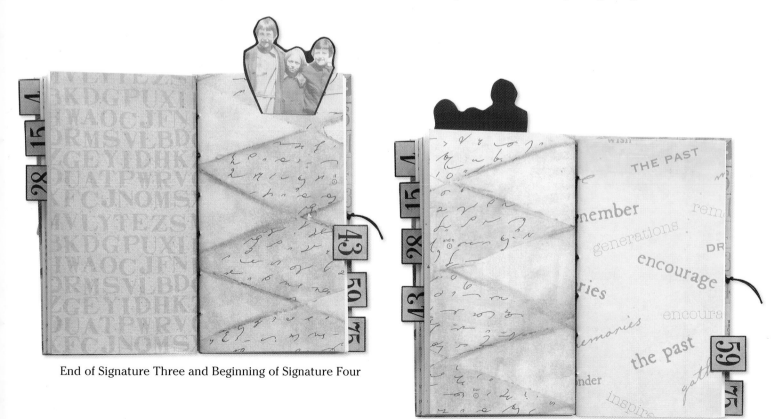

End of Signature Three and Beginning of Signature Four

End of Signature Four and Beginning of Signature Five

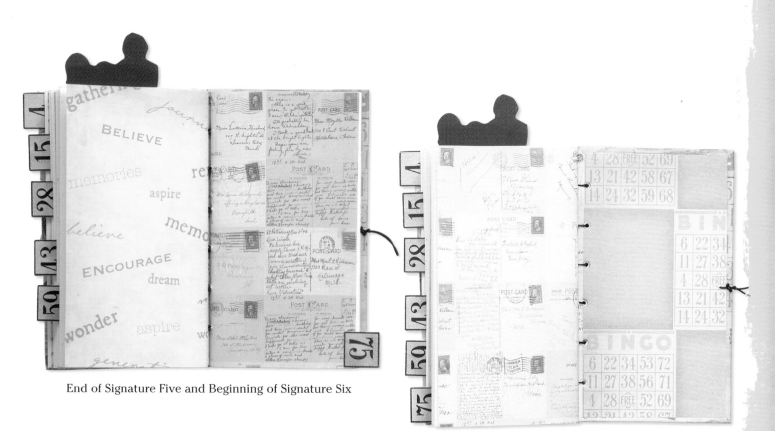

End of Signature Five and Beginning of Signature Six

End of Signature Six and Inside Back Cover

Finish the Book

BOOK CLOSURE:

Drill a hole in the front and back covers, near the edge for a closure. Drill two holes (like a button) in a game piece and attach to the front cover with waxed linen. With the elastic cord, make a small loop and then tie to the back cover. Loop the elastic over the game piece.

Tie two 20" lengths of waxed linen to the top of the binding so that there are 4 equal lengths hanging down. Drill holes in game pieces and tie to the waxed linen to form a tassel. Decorate the journal with more game ephemera.

Fill your book with vintage game pieces, found objects, playing cards from The Ephemera Book, alphabet tiles and poker chips for that popular 3-D look.

Ancestor Star Book

by Beth Cote

This stunning book shows off new art on every side. Add decorative collage papers, photos, tags, mounts and accessories. Showcase the book by tying it open with decorative fibers or thread.

It is fun to alter a children's board book or a small gift book into a beautiful Star shape. The book will fold up for easy storage. Or it can be opened to display on a table in the fascinating Star book shape.

TIP: A book about 6" x 6" is the "perfect size" but any smallish size book will work. Simply adjust the size for the pages you cut.

Pages 1 & 2

Cut out the background from Brushes paper and glue to Tan cardstock. Print out quote on your computer and adhere Super Tape behind quote. Cut quote into strips and adhere to metal tags. Use a jump ring to attach the metal tags together. Center and adhere metal tags to paper with PeelnStick Foam Squares. Spell Family with alphabet beads and string them on waxed linen thread or other button thread. Knot ends. Spray Krylon Suede It! over slide mount and let dry. Spray Black webbing spray over slide mount. Glue strung beads with Ultimate Glue to slide mount. Glue slide mount to vellum tag and both to page 2 of inner star.

How to Make the Book

MATERIALS:

Small book (a children's board book with at least 6 pages, or a gift book with about 40 pages) • *Design Originals* Legacy Collage Papers (#0529 Le Jardin, #0542 Grandfather's Farm, #0543 Brushes, #0547 Dictionary, #0549 Shorthand, #0554 Diamonds) • *Design Originals* Slide Mounts (#0977 White, #0978 Black, #0979 Round) • *Design Originals* Transparency Sheets (#0558 Script, #0560 Objects) • *Design Originals* Ephemera Book #5208 • Cardstock (Brown, Tan) • *Therm O Web* (Super Tape, Peel n Stick foam squares) • Vellum envelopes • *Crafter's Pick*, The Ultimate Glue • *Foofala* Vintage graffiti envelopes • Page clips • Tags (*American Tag*, *Foofala*, *Memory Makers*) • Rubber stamps (*Postmodern Design* City Plan SG2101-F; *Hero Arts* E2096 woven texture, H2141 Manuscript Background) • Ink pads (*Memories* Art Print Brown, Black, Sepia, Ochre; *ColorBox* Cat's Eye Chalk Bisque, Ice Blue, Alabaster) • *Ranger* Blue Smoke Perfect Pearls & Perfect Medium • *Memory Makers* washer words & eyelet charms • *Krylon* Brown Make It Suede & Black Webbing Spray • *Beadery* alphabet beads • Brass eyelets • Masquepen • Fibers

MAKING THE BOOK:

Cut 6 pieces of Brown cardstock the width of your book and 2" shorter than the length of a double spread (or both pages when the book is opened). Cut 6 pieces of Tan cardstock the same width and 1 1/2" shorter than the Brown cardstock.

1. Divide your book into 5 sections and glue the outer quarter of the pages together to make 5 sections. Let dry. **2.** Punch four 1/8" holes along the edge of the cover of your book. Do both the back and front covers. Line them up since we will be lacing the covers together. **3.** Fold all your cardstock in half. **4.** For the large set of 6 cardstock pieces, use super tape and tape the short edges of the cardstock.

5. Adhere the large set of cardstock to the edges of the pages in the book. Your cardstock should be centered, so the folded middle matches the gutter of your book. Tape one edge to one side of the glued section of pages, and then tape the next. Go around the book totally and you should have 6 sections. The book should look like a star now.

6. Collage all six of the inner star pieces of cardstock. (see below) When finished, use super tape to adhere all collaged sheets to the large set of cardstock and page sections around the book. These little collages will sit inside the larger cardstock and need to be adhered like the first set to the edges of the pages. Your cardstock should be centered, so the folded middle matches the gutter of your book. Tape one edge to one side of the glued section of pages and large cardstock, then tape the next. Go around the book totally in all 6 sections.

Glue Pages to Make the 'Star'

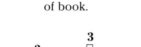
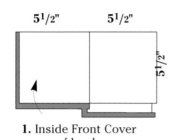

1. Inside Front Cover of book.

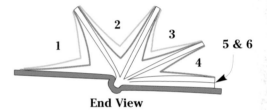

2. Cut 6 pieces of Brown Cardstock.

3. Cut 6 pieces of Tan Cardstock.

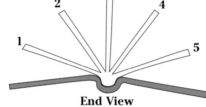
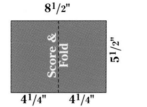

End View

4. Divide book pages into 5 sections. Glue pages together.

End View

5. Glue Brown and Tan cardstock to book covers and between each of the glued sections.

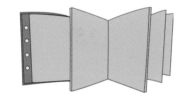

6. Punch holes on front and back covers. Line up holes for lacing.

Top View

7. Open book forms a star shape.

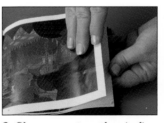

1. Punch evenly spaced holes in front and back covers and set eyelets.

2. Glue pages together in five even sections, putting glue on outer quarter of pages.

3. Line folded cardstock up with edges of book and secure with sticky tape.

4. Secure collaged paper to edges of book on top of the cardstock.

5. Trim the pieces on each cover to clear the eyelets.

6. Use fibers to lace covers together and form star.

Ancestor Star Book

Decorate each page of this fabulous Star shape book in a unique way. Add photos glued to tags, little dangling accents, slide mounts and all the memorabilia you like.

Dedicate the theme of the book to a family member or to a special person in your life. The book will be a keepsake forever.

Pages 3 & 4

Cut collage background from Grandfather's Farm. Cut and glue infant photo from Ephemera book to page 3. Stamp the two small square metal tags with postmark stamp and Black Permanent ink; heat set.

Peel plastic off round slide mount and stamp with City Plan stamp. Wash outside of mount with Walnut ink. Glue "Memories" transparency in slide mount with Ultimate Glue.

Punch two 1/8" holes in bottom of slide mount and hang metal tags. Use foam squares to adhere to page 4.

Pages 5 & 6

Cut Shorthand collage paper to fit Tan cardstock. Rip Dictionary page into pockets and adhere with 1/8" Super Tape.

Decorate tags to put into pockets. Glue a key transparency into a metal tag and attach it to the tag.

Spray Krylon Suede It! over slide mount and let dry. Spray Black webbing spray over slide mount. Glue metal label holder to slide mount. Glue safety pins to sides of holder.

Glue picture to back side of slide mount and adhere to page 6.

Pages 7 & 8

Rip Diamonds paper and Shorthand paper in half and collage to Tan cardstock. With Masquepen, draw an abstract design near ripped edge, and write a quote on the tag. Let dry and paint over words on tag with walnut ink.

Do direct to paper on collage over abstract design with Bisque Chalk Cat's Eye. Let dry. Rub off Blue masking liquid. Glue photo from Ephemera book on page 8. Stamp burlap texture on slide mount with Brown ink; heat set. Rub a bit of Smoke Blue Perfect Pearls over slide mount.

Glue eyeglass transparency off-center and glue photo of woman on outside of slide mount. Use foam squares to adhere to page 7. Glue tag below.

Pages 9 & 10

Cut collage background from Grandfather's Farm and glue to Tan cardstock. Stamp right-hand corner with Postmodern Design stamp using Perfect Medium.

Dust with Smoke Blue Perfect Pearls. Blow off excess pearls. Dust back of slide mount that has tacky glue on it with Smoke Blue Perfect Pearls.

Cut out man's face from Ephemera book and layer with Script transparency. Glue slide mount to vellum tag and tag to page 9. Glue vellum envelope to page 10.

Glue quote on envelope and glue woman in envelope.

Pages 11 & 12

Cut collage background from Le Jardin and glue to Tan cardstock. Glue graffiti pocket to page 11. Hang fibers from tag and glue on quote. Stick in pocket.

Angel Board Book

by Beth Cote

Create a beautiful angel gift for a special friend. Use a children's board book, then add wings and other embellishments.

How to Make the Book

MATERIALS:
Angel Board Book (or cut cardboard wings to fit around a book)
Design Originals Legacy Collage Papers (#0530 Mom's Sewing Box, #0531 Ladies with Hats, #0547 Dictionary, #0549 Shorthand) • Slide Mounts (#0975 Large, #0978 Black) • Transparency Sheets (#0558 Script, #0560 Objects) • Ephemera Book #5208 (pgs. 4, 6 & 7) • *Golden* Gesso • Rubber stamps (*Postmodern Design* Chart of Days; *Love to Stamp* Diamond) • Ink pads (*Memories* Art Print Brown; *Brilliance* Galaxy Gold; *ColorBox* Bisque & Alabaster Cat's Eye Chalk) • *Making Memories* T-pins • *The Beadery* alphabet beads • *Crafter's Pick* Ultimate glue • *Delta* Instant Age varnish • *Wimpole Street* 3" Battenburg lace doily • *Krylon* Gold pen • Small tags • Muslin • Buttons • Masking tape • Fine Sandpaper • 2" rusty lid • 1" faces • Fibers • Found objects

MAKING THE BOOK:
Angel Wings - Sand board book lightly. Dust off the book and work area. • Apply masking tape to the surface of the book wings. Start from the bottom of wings and lay long vertical strips, working up toward the top of wings. Keep ripping and layering tape as you go. Think 'feathers'. • Lightly sponge gesso over wings and let dry. • Wipe with varnish backward (from bottom to top) so varnish settles in the creases and edges. Add another layer of varnish for color if desired. Let dry. • Apply ripped bits of Shorthand paper to inner wings.

Angel on page 13 - Apply Mom's Sewing Box paper and Shorthand paper to the page. • Adhere old Dictionary paper to the head. Glue a small doily on the head. Glue a 2" rusty lid and a 1" face in place. • Take the small slide mount and trace the inside on the first page. With your craft knife, carefully cut through the first page. • On a Black slide mount stamp the Chart of Days with Galaxy Gold ink. Heat set. • Glue a transparency between the mount and the page. Gesso over a bit of muslin. Layer muslin and tape measure on the page. • Glue buttons to page. • Cover small tags with photos from the Ephemera Book or CD. Glue strings around buttons. • Wipe bits of gesso around the page edges. Edge with Bisque and Alabaster Cat's Eye chalk.

Angel on page 14 - Take a large slide mount and trace the inside on the next page. With your craft knife, carefully cut an opening through the page. • On large mount stamp the Diamonds with Brown ink. • Glue a transparency between the large mount and the page. glue and an infant photo to the next page, behind the opening • Cut a small piece of muslin and fray the edges. Paint gesso on it. • Use T-pins to spell a word with beads. Push pins into muslin and add Super Tape over the back. Adhere to page under the picture.

Finish the Angel - With a Gold pen, edge all around angel and wings.

Suggestions - Decorate additional pages as desired. Use a dimensional face on the first page, then use flat faces on additional pages.

Add Texture and Color to the Wings

1. Tear masking tape into 2" to 3" lengths (I like 3/4" wide tape). Starting at the bottom of each wing and the back of the book, overlap tape to create an interesting texture.

2. Paint over masking tape with White Gesso or acrylic paint. You can use a brush, a foam brush, or add texture by applying paint with a palette knife. Allow paint to dry.

3. Apply varnish with a paper towel or a brush. Immediately wipe off excess varnish to age the tape.

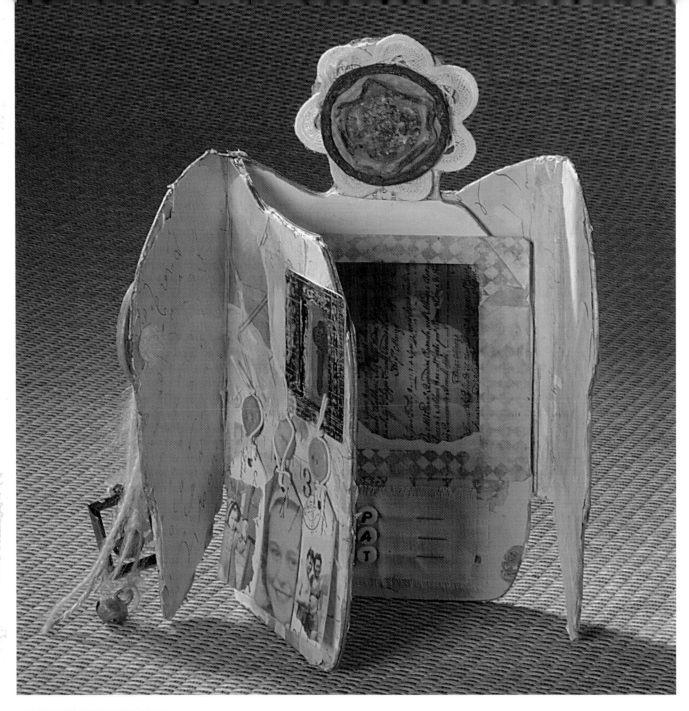

Add a Beautiful Angel Face

Personalize your angel book. These darling books make the perfect baby or first birthday remembrance. Add photos of a young child or baby.

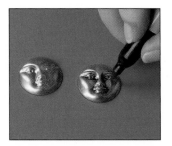

Choose a face that you like. Possibilities include clay, UTEE, brass charms, paper, porcelain and photos.

Use a beautiful brass face. Antique the face with a permanent black marker. Immediately, rub off excess color with an old cloth.

Stamp a pretty face on a round paper tag. Tint the tag with a mixture of instant tea and water. Glue fiber around the rim for hair.

Knead Black clay (polymer or air-dry). Press a clay ball into a face mold or into the back of a face charm. Remove and cure. Add metallic wax. See face on page 12.

Angel Board Book

Angel on page 14 -
Take a large slide mount and trace the inside on the next page. With your craft knife, carefully cut through the page. • On large mount stamp the Diamonds with Brown ink. • Glue a transparency and an infant photo between the large mount and the page. • Cut a small piece of muslin and fray the edges. Paint gesso on it. • Use T-pins to spell a word with beads. Push pins into muslin and add Super Tape over the back. Adhere to the page under the picture.

Board Book Size

Use a children's board book about 4" wide x 5 1/2" tall to place in the center of the Angel Wings and Book Cover Pattern.

TIP:
Adjust the size of the Angel Wings to fit larger or smaller books.

TIP:
Cut and round the edges of the board book if desired, or leave the corners square.

Score and Fold along the dash lines.

**Angel Wings
and
Book Cover Pattern**

Cut this piece out of stiff board.

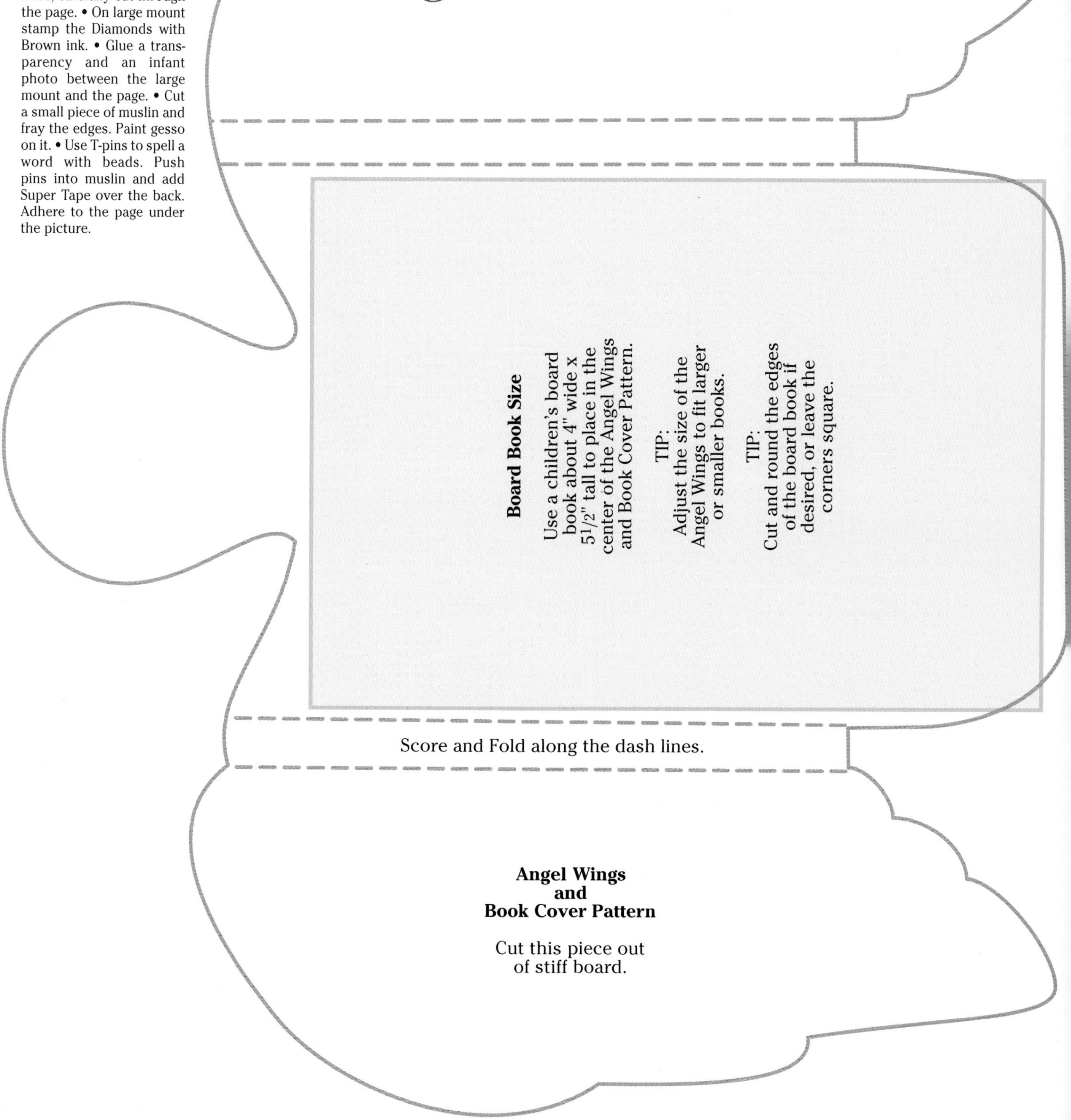

1. Heat CD with heat gun. Punch hole. Repeat for all CDs, making sure holes are aligned.

2. Using a CD as a pattern, trace onto leather to make a cover. Mark the hole.

3. Cut a 2" square hole in the leather with a craft knife.

4. Glue Map paper to the back of the leather. Cover with a scrap of paper. Use a brayer to burnish paper to leather.

5. Embellish with stamps, papers, charms or ephemera.

CD Deco Book

by Lynda Musante

Take recycling to new levels when you turn old CDs into astonishing art. This CD deco is portable, stores in a small space, and will make a beautiful conversation piece for your coffee table or desk.

This sample is a travel journal. Let it guide your imagination toward your own theme. A "What I Love About You" deco would make a unique gift for anyone on your list. Take a journey out of the box and create something wonderful today.

Create this clever eclectic travel journal with leftover computer CDs. Add bits of travel memorabilia to preserve your memories of a special journey. Decorate each page made from a CD with paints, textures and paper ephemera. Hold the booklet together with a notebook ring decorated with fibers, tags, and charms.

Listed throughout are the supplies the designers used. Substitute your favorite stamp images, colors, papers, charms, and ephemera.

How to Make the CDs Book

MATERIALS:
Tandy Leather Gold Soft Cowhide Suede • Contact cement • Japanese Screw punch with 2 mm tip • Rubber brayer • Heat gun • CDs
TIP: Use contact cement in a well-ventilated area.

INSTRUCTIONS:
Heat a CD with a heat gun. While CD is still quite warm, punch a hole. Repeat for each CD, making sure the holes are aligned. • Use contact cement to glue papers to CDs. Also, when making the covers, use contact cement to glue leather to paper, or leather to CD.

Cover the CDs with Paper:

MATERIALS:
Design Originals Legacy Papers (#0546 Currency, #0547 Dictionary, #0548 Passport, #0553 Map) • $1/4$" round hole punch • Rubber brayer • Contact cement

INSTRUCTIONS:
Trace around the CD on paper. Trace the punched hole. • Cut the paper on the traced line. Punch a hole on the marked location. • Adhere cut out paper to CD with contact cement, aligning punched holes. • Cover with a piece of scrap paper and burnish paper to CD with brayer. Burnish each time you glue to a CD.

Make the Leather Cover:

MATERIALS:
Design Originals Legacy Papers (#0548 Passport, #0553 Map) • *Tandy Leather* Gold Soft Cowhide Suede Leather • *Making Memories* (Eyelet Alphabet, eyelet tool) • Hammer • *ColorBox* Fluid Chalk Ink (Chestnut Roan, Bisque) • *Nostalgiques by Rebecca Sower* Black typewriter letters • *Krylon* Silver Leafing Pen • Wooden game piece letters (T, E) • Japanese screw punch with 2 mm tip • Postage stamps • $1/4$" circle punch

INSTRUCTIONS:
Use contact cement when gluing to leather. Trace around the CD on leather. Mark the punched hole. Use scissors to cut the leather on the traced line. Punch a hole on marked location. • Use a stipple brush to pounce Fluid Chalk Ink in Chestnut Roan and Bisque onto the smooth side of the leather. • Glue the letter "T" game piece to the leather about 2" left of the punched hole. Add a Black typewriter "R" sticker. Punch a hole for the letter "A" with a Japanese Screw Punch, and use the eyelet setting tool to set the letter. • Add a Black typewriter "V" sticker. Glue the letter "E" game piece in place. Use a Japanese Screw Punch to make a hole for the letter "L", and set it with the eyelet setting tool. • Use a ruler to measure a 2" square as shown in photo. Cut out the square with a craft knife. Glue Legacy Map paper to the back side of the leather. Punch a hole in the paper through the hole punched in the leather. Use a craft knife to cut out the square. Use a Silver Leafing Pen to highlight the edges of the cutout opening. Cut out small motifs from Legacy Passport paper. Glue small motifs and postage stamps as shown in photo.

Assemble the Book:

MATERIALS:
Design Originals Legacy Paper (#0548 Passport) • *Tandy Leather* (Turquoise & Beige Velvet Jewelry Lace) • *Making Memories* (Vellum Rectangle Tags; Metal rim tags) • *JudiKins* Diamond Glaze • *EK Success* Monet Adornments fibers • *Avery* (Disappearing Color Glue Stick; Metal Rimmed Tags) • Silver 8mm Beads • Laminate sample • Metal charms • Ribbon

INSTRUCTIONS:
Stack up decorated CDs, aligning punched holes. Cut several 10" lengths of different fibers, ribbon and velvet jewelry lace. Fold lengths in half. Insert one length of velvet jewelry lace through punched CD holes. Insert one end of lace through loop of folded fibers and secure with a square knot. Attach metal-rimmed tags, stamped vellum rectangle and embellished laminate sample to different fibers with knots. Add beads and charms to additional fibers. Knot to secure.

Use your leftover CDs to create a clever book.

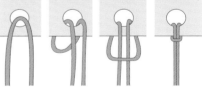

Lark's Head Knot
Use this simple knot to add tags
with string and fibers.

1. Cut decorative paper to fit the tag. Adhere with glue.

2. Brush with Diamond Glaze to seal the surface.

3. Add fibers to small ring with Lark's Head knot.

4. Assemble fibers and pages of book onto large ring.

CD Deco Book

Carte Postale Page
by Lynda Musante

Highlight a favorite postcard and quote with this embellished page.

MATERIALS:
Design Originals Legacy Collage Paper (#0546 Currency) • *Nostalgiques Postal Pieces* sticker • Poem "The Road Not Taken" by Robert Frost (1874-1963) • *Ah That's Great* tape (ATG) • *Curiously Sticky* tape • Tiny marbles • Watch parts • Postal stamps • Glue stick

INSTRUCTIONS:
Trace around the CD on Currency paper. Trace the punched hole. Cut out paper and punched hole. • Glue Currency paper to CD. • Peel and stick postcard image to CD as shown. Write a message on the postcard. • Print the poem, tear out and glue to CD. Use ATG tape to adhere tiny marbles as shown. Use a glue stick to adhere postal stamps. Use Curiously Sticky tape to adhere watch parts.

Leftover CDs from your computer make great pages for deco books.

Foreign Travels Page
by Lynda Musante

Showcase a special poem or quotation that captures the theme of your book.

MATERIALS:
Design Originals Legacy Collage Paper (#0548 Passport) • Computer generated font • Fleur de Lis stamp • *ColorBox* Ink Pads (Chestnut Roan Chalk, Yellow Cadmium Chalk, Black Pigment) • Metallic acrylic paint (Orange, Gold, Bronze, Purple) • Text "When you travel" by Clifton Fadiman (1904 -) • Black detail embossing powder • *Ah That's Great* tape (ATG) • *Curiously Sticky* tape • Tiny marbles • Watch parts • Stipple brush • Heat gun

INSTRUCTIONS:
Make a background paper using a computer generated print and a Chestnut Roan fleur de lis stamp. Use a stipple brush to add paint. • Trace around CD on paper. Trace the punched hole. Cut out paper and punched hole. • Glue paper to CD. • Tear out the poem. Brush the torn edges of the poem against the Black pigment ink and pour Black embossing powder on the edges. Tap off the excess and melt the powder with a heat gun. • Tear out a larger piece of collage Passport paper. Mount the poem to the Passport paper and glue the paper to the CD.

Age Background Paper and Quotes

1. Stipple paint onto the background paper.

2. Rub edges of saying on Black embossing pad.

3. Add the Black embossing powder.

4. Age the paper with chalk ink, glue to CD.

Happy Travels
by Tracia Williams

Have fun with hidden messages... the passport records notes and the envelope fold out to reveal photos or notes.

MATERIALS:
Design Originals Legacy Collage Paper (#0548 Passport) • Reduced copies of vintage papers and postcards • Old stamps • *Jolee's By You* passport and money • Small glass bottle • 24" wire • Assorted beads • Chinese coin • Small key charm • Fibers • Awl • Self-healing mat • Metallic gold micro beads • Large manila tag • *Anna Griffin* background stamp • *Ranger* Coffee Archival Ink.

TIP: Anchor bottle in place with glue before wiring.

INSTRUCTIONS:
Lay the CD on passport paper. Trace twice. Cut out with scissors. Cover the CD with paper. Let dry. • Punch a single hole with hole punch for loop that holds the CDs together. • Opposite, punch two small holes with the awl. Fill the bottle with micro beads. Glue to CD with craft glue. Wire the bottle to the CD. Add beads and key charm. Twist the ends of the wire. • Stamp tag. Let dry. Fold into thirds to make the brown envelope. Glue images to the inside of the tag envelope. Glue folded tag to the CD. Add fibers and Chinese coin to the tag. • Glue stamps, vintage images, passport and money in place. Open the ring on the deco book and add page.

Bon Voyage Page
by Tracia Williams

Fill this page, like your travels, with good wishes and happy thoughts.

MATERIALS:
Design Originals Legacy Collage Paper (#0548 Passport) • Reduced copies of vintage map • Excerpt from Robert Frost poem "The Road Not Taken" printed on transparency • *Nostalgiques by Rebecca Sower* Black typewriter letters • Double-stick tape

INSTRUCTIONS:
Cover the CD with collage paper. • Glue map in place. Position poem and attach with double-stick tape. Glue stickers in place. Write a note and sign your name.

Destinations Page
by Billie Worrell

Try bleaching on this page. It is really fun.

MATERIALS:
Black gel paper • Yellow cardstock • *Delta* Sobo Glue • *Rubber Stampede* (World Travel rubber stamp kit; wood handle stamp A2530D Nostalgic Ship; Pigment Ink Pads: Purple, Gold, Fuchsia, Turquoise, Emerald Green) • *Ranger* Pumpkin Pie ink pad • *Clorox* Ultra Advantage bleach • Computer printed travel quotes • *DMD* shipping tag • Metal tag • *Making Memories Details* brad • Round silk sponge • Squeeze bottle with tip • 1/4" circle punch

INSTRUCTIONS:
Use a round silk sponge to apply all colors of ink to paper. Glue paper to CD and trim. Edge with Purple ink. • Print travel quote onto Yellow cardstock, tear and edge with ink. Add the metal tag to the quote with a brad and glue onto the CD. • Use desired stamps from the World Travel Stamp Kit and Nostalgic Ship and stamp onto Black gel paper using the bleaching technique. • Tear out the images. Edge with Gold ink and glue as shown. • Use hole punch and punch out over original hole.

TIP: Use bleach in a well-ventilated area.

BLEACHING TECHNIQUE:
Pour a small amount of bleach onto a plate. Dip the stamp into the bleach. • Stamp onto Black gel paper. Clean the stamp. • Repeat until you have the desired number of images.

CD Deco Book

Go Page
by Lynda Musante

Decorate a library pocket to hold an assortment of tags and travel memorabilia.

MATERIALS:
Design Originals Legacy Papers (#0553 Map, #0547 Dictionary) • *Making Memories* (Mini Square Gold Brads) • Library pocket • *Avery* Disappearing Color glue stick • *Halcraft* 1/4" wide Curiously Sticky tape • *ColorBox* (Fluid Chalk Ink: Bisque, Ice Blue, Wisteria; Black pigment ink pad • *DMD* shipping tags • *USArtquest* Perfect fx embossing tiles • *Fiskars* (Softouch Micro-Tip Scissors; 1/4" circle punch) • Clear detail embossing powder • CD • *Tin Can Mail* alphabet stamps • Metal globe charm • Stipple brushes

INSTRUCTIONS:
Place CD on Legacy Dictionary paper. Lightly trace around the CD with a pen. Trace the punched hole. Cut out paper on traced line. Punch hole on marked location. Adhere Map paper to CD with contact cement, aligning punched holes. • Cover with a piece of scrap paper and burnish paper to CD with brayer. • Cover library pocket with Legacy Map paper, adhering with glue stick. Anchor the pocket corners with tiny square brads. Use Curiously Sticky tape to attach library pocket to CD and Globe charm to pocket front. • Pounce Ice Blue and Wisteria Fluid Chalk ink onto game piece. • Stamp "GO" with Black pigment ink. Pour clear embossing powder on game piece. Tap off excess and melt powder with heat gun. • Attach game piece to pocket with Curiously Sticky tape.

MAKING THE TAGS:
Cut 4 shipping tags 1" longer than the pocket. One tag will be completed and signed by each designer. For the first tag, stipple Ice Blue and Wisteria Fluid Chalk ink onto tag. Pour clear embossing powder onto the tag, tapping off excess and melting the powder with a heat tool. Print a poem on a transparency. Attach the poem to the tag with double-stick tape. Insert the tag into pocket.

To make the large beaded donut, wrap with thread loaded with seed beads.

Map to Happy Land Page
by Kim Ballor

Mark your route with a beaded path. Use this page to record a vacation or the route to a new home.

MATERIALS:
Road Map • Size 11 seed beads, colors to match the map • Beading needle • Beading thread • Tags, charms, and beads for dangles • Double-stick tape

INSTRUCTIONS:
Cut two pieces of map the size of the CD. Glue together so you are stitching through two layers of paper. • Using a beading needle, back stitch seed beads to cover the rivers and highways on the map. • String tags and beads and stitch as dangles at the top of map. • Glue finished paper to CD, Glue another circle of map to the back of the CD. • Print caption on scrap paper and glue to finished CD.

Drive to HAPPYLAND
And throw your keys
In the river

Suitcases Page
by Billie Worrell

This page reminds us that suitcases need tags. Label yours with your favorite travel quote.

MATERIALS:
Black gel paper • Blue vellum • *Delta* Sobo Glue • *Rubber Stampede* (World Travel rubber stamp kit; Pigment Ink Pads: Purple, Gold, Fuchsia, Emerald Green, Turquoise) • *Ranger* Pumpkin Pie Ink Pad • *Ultra Clorox* Advantage bleach • Computer printed travel quotes • *DMD* shipping tag • Fibers • Round silk sponge • Squeeze bottle with tip • 1/4" circle punch

TIP: Use bleach in a well-ventilated area.

INSTRUCTIONS:
Pour the bleach into a squeeze bottle and create lines on Blue vellum by squeezing gently. Let dry. Glue onto a CD and trim. • Print a travel quote onto White paper, tear and edge with Purple ink. • Sponge desired colors of inks onto a tag and add fibers. • Stamp the suitcase from World Travel Kit onto Black gel paper using the bleach technique and tear out. Edge with Gold ink. • Glue the tag, quote and image onto CD as shown. • Use the hole punch and punch out over the original hole.

1. Stipple background paper with ink.

2. Stamp onto scrap paper to lighten ink, then stamp background paper.

3. Unroll ATG tape into squiggly line. Pour on tiny beads.

4. Glue torn images to page.

5. Attach embellishments.

Create Original Background Paper

by Lynda Musante

Make your own papers for little books and other crafts. You can even frame these pages and display your unique art.

When layering color, be sure to work lightest to darkest. Use color sparingly, as more can always be added.

DIRECT TO PAPER BACKGROUNDS:
Tape the map to work surface. Begin by pouncing a stipple brush on Bisque ink pad. Pounce the stipple brush on the map, creating loose drifts of color. Follow up with Ice Blue and Wisteria inks. Sparingly add Chestnut Roan ink. • Add stamped images, frequently blotting initially inked stamp on scrap paper to create a lighter imprint. Vary the angle of the stamped image and the color used when stamping. • Unroll a length of ATG tape in the upper left quadrant of the map, unrolling in a 4" wiggly line. Pour tiny marbles over the ATG tape, pressing the marbles onto the tape. Repeat in the lower left and lower right quadrants of the map. • Stamp an image with black pigment ink onto an embossing tile. Pour black embossing powder on the image. Tap off the excess and melt powder with heat tool. Glue tile in place using PPA. • Attach postage stamps, domino, key, metal charms, and watch parts with Curiously Sticky tape. • Use a stipple brush to pounce Red pigment ink from Aurora ink pad onto skeletonized leaf. Pour clear embossing powder on the leaf. Tap off the excess and melt powder with heat tool. Glue leaf and ribbon with PPA. • Tear edges around Black and White image. Use stipple brush to pounce Bisque ink onto the image. Pour clear embossing powder over ink. Tap off excess and melt powder with heat tool. Attach image with glue stick.

Vintage Greetings Book

by Dorothy Egan

Gather your greeting cards to display your collection in this beautiful book. Have fun with all the flaps and surprises this book has to offer.

How to Make the Book

Cut office supply folders to make the pages needed for the cover and inside. Use a size suitable for your cards. The sample uses 6" x 5 1/2" • Use a 1/4" hole punch to make holes 2 1/2" apart on one of the 5 1/2" edges. Glue the reinforcement circles around the holes.

MATERIALS:

Design Originals Legacy Collage paper (#0550 TeaDye Script) • *Plaid* FolkArt Metallic paints (Silver Sterling, Blue Sapphire, Taupe, Inca Gold) • 1/2" flat brush • Two 3" doilies • Vintage tatting • Jewelry • Postage stamps • Greeting card

INSTRUCTIONS:

Use a 1/2" flat brush to paint Silver Sterling so that the surface is almost covered. Apply the paint randomly with a swirling motion, using enough paint to allow easy blending. • Add Blue Sapphire and blend to create a soft color. Add tints of Taupe and Inca Gold.

Let dry, then repeat on the back side of the page. • Use TeaDye Script paper to create a pocket for the card (see below). Fold under 1/4" on all sides. Set aside. • To make the doily less flimsy, glue two 3" doilies together so the patterns match. Cut away the center.

Position the card between the doilies and the pocket. Adjust the placement so the doily fits over the card design you want to feature. • Set the card aside and glue the doily to the pocket. Cut a circle in the pocket. Position and glue the pocket to the page.

Glue tatting around the opening. Glue vintage jewelry at the bottom of the circle. Slide the card in place.

1. Cut pages to desired size. Use a 1/4" hole punch to make 2 holes.

2. Reinforce all the holes on both sides with paper reinforcement rings.

3. Score the pages with dull edge of craft knife.

4. Fold pocket for front and back cover. Punch hole and attach to cover.

Celebrations Page
by Dorothy Egan

MATERIALS:
Computer generated font • Tissue paper • Glue stick • *Mod Podge* • Postage stamps • Gold Leafing pen

INSTRUCTIONS:
Use your computer to create a background paper by typing the names of special occasions in a variety of fonts with light blue ink. Repeat to fill most of the page. • Cut tissue slightly smaller than printer paper. • Use glue stick to make a line across the top of the paper. Glue tissue to paper. • Print the special occasions words onto tissue. Tear to fit the deco page and glue to the page with Mod Podge. When dry, decorate with postage stamps and write the story of your deco. Edge the pages with Gold Leafing pen.

Satin Oval Page   by Dorothy Egan

MATERIALS:
Vintage card with satin oval • Stamp pads (*Memories* Rainbow, *StazOn* Royal Purple) • Blue patterned vellum • 4 Gold eyelets • Eyelet setter • Gold Leafing pen • Deckle-edge scissors • 1/2" wide sheer ribbon • Double-stick tape • Vintage button • Cut out butterfly • Old photo • Foam sponge

SATIN OVAL INSTRUCTIONS:
Use a sponge to rub the page with blue and purple inks. • Use deckle-edge scissors to cut the padded oval from the card with a 1/4" border. • Cut vellum to fit the page. Cut an oval in the vellum to fit the satin cutout. • Center the satin cutout and glue to the page. Attach vellum to the page with eyelets. • Add decorations and line the edges with a Gold leafing pen.

Mother's Day Page   by Dorothy Egan
Preserve the sentimental words of a special card.

MATERIALS:
Design Originals Legacy Collage Paper (#0526 Two Ladies) • Stamp pads (*Memories* Rainbow, *Staz-On* Royal Purple) • Gold Leafing pen • Deckle-edge scissors • 1 1/4" wide sheer ribbon • Verse from greeting card • Double-stick tape • Spray adhesive • Fibers • Micro beads in purple tones • Leaf button • *Plaid* Royal Coat Dimensional Magic

INSTRUCTIONS:
Cut collage paper to fit the page. Rub the collage paper with Blue and Purple inks. Use spray adhesive to attach collage paper to the page. • Cut a ribbon to fit diagonally across the page and attach it with double-sided tape. • Cut out a card verse with deckle scissors and paint the edges with a Gold pen. • Glue verse to the page. Glue fibers and button to the page. Use Dimensional Magic to attach micro beads.

How Do I Love Thee?   by Beth Wheeler
A doily envelope provides an elegant home for a treasured Valentine.

MATERIALS:
Pink handmade paper • Square doily • Reproduced vintage valentine • 1/8" Pink ribbon • Heart charms • Watercolor paper • Waxed paper

INSTRUCTIONS:
Tear a piece of handmade paper to roughly match the size of the book's page. • Fold three corners of the doily to the center, overlapping slightly. Slip a piece of waxed paper inside the overlap and glue. Weight until dry. • Glue envelope on the page. Glue charms and transfers to valentine and envelope. • Insert valentine into doily envelope.

Vintage Greetings Book

A Gift of Love Page
by Tracia Williams

Celebrate an anniversary or wedding with classic symbols of lasting romance...keys, hearts, lace, beads, and butterflies.

MATERIALS:
Design Originals Legacy Collage Paper (#0541 Report Card) • Vintage postcard • Vintage wedding gift card • Assorted charms, beads, lace, costume jewelry, fibers, ribbons • Foil butterfly • Brown ink pad • Sponge • 18" white ribbon

INSTRUCTIONS:
Cut out report card paper to cover the deco page. • Score and fold the postcard 3/4" from the bottom. Glue the fold to the bottom of the page. • Fold the postcard back. On the back side, glue a piece of lace as shown. • Print a message and tear it to fit the back of the postcard. Sponge the edges with Brown ink. Glue the message in place. • Position the small gift card so it is hidden by the postcard flap. Add a foil butterfly, foil flower, and ribbon tied in a small shoestring style bow. • Add lace, beads, and other vintage ephemera using Dimensional Magic. • Tie 18" of ribbon in loops to the string that holds the book together. Tie charms to the ends of the ribbon.

Just a Note
by Tracia Williams

Pages don't have to be elaborate to be meaningful. Add a personal touch to your deco with this message space.

MATERIALS:
Design Originals Legacy Collage paper (#0541 Report Card) • Brown marker

INSTRUCTIONS:
Cover the deco page with Report Card paper. Write a note.

Postcard and Lace Page
by Dorothy Egan

Soft color and a music background give a sentimental feel while lace holds a postcard in place.

MATERIALS:
Plaid FolkArt Metallic paints (Silver Sterling, Blue Sapphire, Taupe, Inca Gold) • 1/2" flat brush • 9" of 1 1/2" sheer ribbon and 3/4" wide beaded sheer ribbon • Double-sided tape • Vintage postcard and postage stamps • Light Blue tissue paper • Music stamp • *Brilliance* Gold ink pad • Gold embossing powder • Heat gun • ModPodge

INSTRUCTIONS:
With the flat brush, apply paint to the page randomly in a circular motion, using enough paint to allow easy blending. Apply Silver Sterling so that surface is almost covered. Add Blue Sapphire and blend to create a soft color. Add tints of Taupe and Inca Gold. • Stamp tissue with the music stamp and emboss. Repeat until the design will cover the page. • Tear tissue to fit and attach to the page with ModPodge. Glue stamps in place. Layer the ribbons and attach diagonally across the page with double-sided tape. Slide the postcard under the ribbon and spot glue it in place.

Sometimes romantic, sometimes sweet, but always a delight. Vintage cards make wonderful little books.

Hickory Dickory Dock!

by Dorothy Egan

This embellished envelope has birthday wishes tucked inside. It also hides a door mouse.

MATERIALS:
Design Originals Collage Legacy Paper (#0551 Legacy Words) • Ivory parchment paper • *Brilliance* Taupe ink pad • *Just For Fun* (keyhole stamp, postal stamps) • Vintage card • Cancelled postage stamps • Lace • Tatting • Photos • Small brass key • Spray adhesive

INSTRUCTIONS:
Cut the collage paper to fit the deco page and attach with spray adhesive. • Stamp keyhole design onto a scrap of ivory paper with taupe ink. Cut out and set aside. • Use the original envelope or make an envelope from ivory paper. • Because this card had a mouse featured on it, we cut a mouse hole shaped opening in the envelope to fit the card design. The stamped keyhole created the flap over the mouse hole to make a door. • Fold the envelope flap backwards toward the front of the envelope. • Glue the envelope to the page. • Stamp the envelope with the postal stamps using Taupe ink. • Glue photos, lace and tatting to the flap. Glue stamps and key to the page. • Insert the card into envelope.

My Favorite Holiday

by Beth Wheeler

Capture the spirit of your favorite day with vintage memorabilia and beautiful watercolor paper!

MATERIALS:
Reproduced vintage valentine • Heart charm • Gold leafing pen • Variegated background paper • Burgundy cardstock

INSTRUCTIONS:
Tear variegated background paper and glue to deco page. • Mat the valentine on Burgundy cardstock and glue in place. • Glue a heart charm in place and write a message.

Coasters Book

by Tracia Williams

Decorate drink coasters from your favorite restaurant with memorabilia honoring the women in your life.

Front Cover
Glue the title. Add embellishments to the front cover.

How to Make the Book

MATERIALS:
Cardboard drink coasters • Cardstock • *Plaid* Dimensional Magic • Assorted buttons, charms, old watch pieces and keys • *All Night Media* Lace rubber stamp • *Ranger* Archival Coffee ink • Assorted vintage images • Lemon juice • Heat gun • Fibers • 2 binder rings • Tiny glass beads • Computer printed or stamped verse and title • *Loew Cornell* watercolors

TIP: Cardboard drink coasters come in a variety of shapes and sizes. These make the perfect cover for a deco.

INSTRUCTIONS:
Lay a coaster over cardstock and trace 4 times. Cut out and glue to both sides of two coasters. Punch holes in coaster for the binder rings, creating a book. • Stamp all 4 sides of the coasters with the lace stamp and Coffee ink. Let dry. Softly add washes of watercolors to lace.

MAKE THE BOOK:
Add binder rings, then wrap fibers on them and tie.

Inside Front Cover
Grandma Ruth taught me to play bingo and sew. We made lemon pies and cut out cookies. She loved to laugh.

I will never forget her.
For this small book, add game pieces and vintage images that have been reduced in size.

INSIDE PAGES:
The inside pages are made by cutting and gluing cardstock together. Stamp and color the pages. Add vintage images to the first page and glue text on the reverse side.

Poem Page

Cover the page with Faces of Friends paper. Print a personal message on parchment cardstock. Trim the message into tag shape to fit the page. Punch a hole then stick on Brown hole reinforcement. Thread fibers through the hole in the tag. Glue the tag and a piece of lace to the page.

Fold-Out Page *by Barbara Matthiessen*

Wonderful women teach us to believe in ourselves. This page recalls the women who have helped find my path.

MATERIALS:
Design Originals Legacy Collage Papers (#0526 Two Ladies, #0537 Faces of Friends) • Parchment cardstock • Two 1" to 2" photocopies of black and white photos • *All Night Media* Anna Griffin rubber stamps (Swirl Motif, Georgian Cartouche) • Clearsnap Ancient Page Sienna ink pad • Three gold eyelets • 10" heavy lace • *Adornaments* fibers • Glue stick • White glue • Deckle-edge scissors • 1/8" hole punch • Paper reinforcement • Computer generated script or Brown ink pen.

INSTRUCTIONS:
Cut pieces of Legacy Collage paper a little bigger than the Deco page. Trim all the edges with deckle scissors. Cover the Deco page front and back. Glue a strip of "Wonderful Women" text to the bottom front of the page. Re-punch the holes.

MAKING THE FOLD OUT:
Using the same paper, cut a 2" x 8" vertical strip and accordion fold it into thirds. • Use Sienna ink for all coloring and stamping. Stamp cartouche around a small face from the Faces of Friends paper and tear out. Stamp motifs randomly on the 2" wide strip. • Tear pieces for photo mats from the remaining collage paper slightly larger than the photocopies and stamped face. Stamp the mats with Sienna ink. Layer and glue the stamped and inked papers down the strip away from the folds. Position the lace down one side of the strip and attach with White glue. • Reinforce the bottom eyelet hole by gluing a small square of scrap paper to the backside, bottom center of strip. Attach eyelets at the bottom of the strip. Thread fibers through the eyelet. Fold up the strip to close; pull the fibers to open the book. • Use 2 eyelets at the top to attach the strip to the page.

Open in the center to reveal the photo.

Door Page

To make a door page, trace the page shape (double the width) onto Two Ladies paper. • Cut out the shape and fold a flap in on each side. Add a photo inside. Glue lace where the doors meet. Glue a button to the lace.

Make Pages Easy-to-Decorate

1. After paper images are on a surface, add lines of Dimensional Magic.

2. Next, add larger pieces of embellishments.

3. Add smaller pieces of embellishment and sprinkle with the micro beads.

Back Cover

by Tracia Williams

The back cover is made the same way as the front cover. A verse has been added to describe the theme of the book. Glue buttons around the verse.

Leaf Page

Glue layered Green papers and vintage photo on the page. Randomly stamp images in Gray ink. • Make the branch by cutting seven lengths of wire about a foot long. On each, slide one leaf bead to the center and fold over, bringing ends of wire together. Twist the wire together to form the branch.

Partway up each branch, slide on another leaf and continue twisting. Make seven branches and twist them together forming the larger end of the branch. Trim to the same length. • Punch six tiny holes in the paper so you can thread wire through the holes to couch the stem in place. Glue the paper to the deco page.

Story Page

Glue Green papers directly to deco page. Stamp and glue the story and ephemera on top.

Femme Deco

by Kim Ballor

Pastoral pages present Kim's great grandmother with her photo. Her story is in both French and English.

MATERIALS:
Assorted Green papers • Photocopy of ancestor and her story • *All Night Media* (Swirl Motif and Ornamental Letters and Numbers rubber stamps; Gray ink pad) • 15-17 glass leaf beads • Thin Copper craft wire • Glue • Gathered family ephemera.

INSTRUCTIONS:
For all 3 pages, cut Green paper the size of the deco pages.

Make a book with your friends. Create a book that includes the women who have influenced your life for the better.

Signature Page

Everyone should sign their name here for the signature page.

Photo Page

Write a story and print out on cardstock. Glue the story and the photo to the page. Glue buttons around the photo.

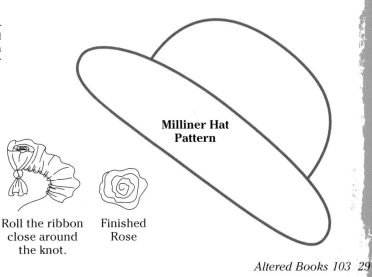

Helen FitzGerald was my father's mother. She died when I was young and what I know about her comes from my father's stories. Though financially poor, she was rich in talent. Pop said she could look at a fancy dress or hat in the store window and copy it to perfection. Every Halloween she made costumes for all the neighborhood. How I wish I had known her....... *Chris 2003*

Milliner Extraordinaire
by Chris Malone

Grandmother was rich in talent. She could look at a fancy hat and copy it to perfection.

MATERIALS:
Brown advertisement paper • Watercolor paper • Cream cardstock • Light Brown and Gray inks • *Contessa* rayon/silk yarns (Luggage, Butterscotch) • 10" of 5/8" wide Cream wire-edged ribbon • 2 feathers (Cream, Light Brown) • 8" of Brown dyed silk ribbon • Scrap of vintage lace • Vintage brass and pearl button, shank removed • 6" of 26 gauge Gold wire • 6 small pearls • 2 tiny brass charms • Brass scissor charm • Copy of old photo • 4 small White buttons • Computer generated font • Sponge applicator • Embroidery needle • Glue • Toothpick

INSTRUCTIONS:
Glue advertisement paper to pages for background. • Tear 2 1/2" x 2 3/4" rectangle from watercolor paper. Apply Brown ink to the edges of the paper and add touches of Gray. • Use pattern to draw hat on paper. Outline the brim with stem stitch and medium Brown yarn. Fill in with Light Brown ink using finger or sponge applicator. Satin stitch the crown of the hat with lighter yarn. • Glue paper to the page.

TO MAKE RIBBON ROSE:
Tie a knot at one end of the ribbon. Pull one wire to tightly gather one side of the ribbon. Roll the ribbon close around the knot, then in looser rounds until a rose shape is formed. Wrap a wire around the knot to secure. Trim. Use fingers to shape and press down on rose.

TO FINISH:
Clip feathers to 1" and glue to the hat. Glue a ribbon rose over the feather ends. • Tie silk ribbon into a bow. Tuck and glue the bow under the edge of the rose. • Thread pearls and small charm onto gold wire. Twist the wire around a toothpick to curl. Arrange lace, wire, button and remaining charm on the corner of the paper and glue in place.

Milliner Hat Pattern

How to Make a Ribbon Rose

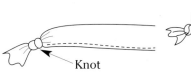

Tie knot at one end of ribbon.

Pull one wire to tightly gather one side of the ribbon.

Roll the ribbon close around the knot.

Finished Rose

I love little children,
and it is not a slight thing
when they, who are
fresh from God, love us.
— Charles Dickens

Accordion Book

by Barbara Matthiessen

Celebrate joy with a beautiful book folded from a long sheet of paper.

How to Make the Accordion Book

MATERIALS:
Design Originals Legacy Collage Papers (#0538 Peter's Dreams, #0540 Skates, #0544 Bingo, and #0549 Shorthand) • Parchment cardstock • White copy paper • Black and white photocopies • Rubber stamps (*Uptown Design* #13310 I Love Little Children; *All Night Media* Ornamental Letters & Numbers) • *Clearsnap* Ancient Page Sienna ink pad • Opaque shrink plastic • *Krylon* 18 kt Metallic Gold Leafing Pen • Colored pencils • 2 yards Ivory $3/8$" ribbon • Brass heart-shaped button • Double-stick tape.• Computer generated text • Heat gun

MAKING THE BOOK:
Cut Peter's Dream collage and roller skate pages in half widthwise. Back collage sheet with cardstock cut to size. Make accordion pages from roller skate paper following instructions. Attach the pages to the cover using double stick tape on front tab. Cut 3 heart accordion booklets from script paper following instructions.

How to Handtint Photos

1. Use a colored pencil to shade the photo, starting with the lightest colors first.

2. Continue coloring the photo.

3. Use a pencil eraser to shade the colors.

Front Cover

by Barbara Matthiessen

Scale the photocopies to fit the cover and inside pages on one heart accordion booklet. Use colored pencils on the front photocopy following instructions. • Stamp saying on copy paper using Sienna ink. Computer print the name with Brown ink. Tear or cut around the computer printing. Rub Sienna ink directly from ink pad onto all paper edges. • Glue the center of an 18" ribbon to the center back of heart booklet. Use a glue stick to adhere paper layers in place. Tie ribbons in bows. Glue the heart button in place.

1. Fold edges of paper down.

2. Unfold tab on right, run glue stick down tab. Place second paper on top of glue and press.

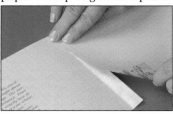

3. Fold 1" tab on other end of paper. Trim 1/2" off tab.

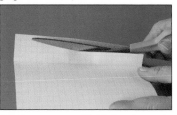

4. Turn over. Fold both ends into center.

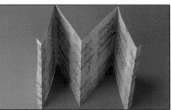

5. Fold center seam toward you, accordion style.

Accordion Hearts Page

by Barbara Matthiessen

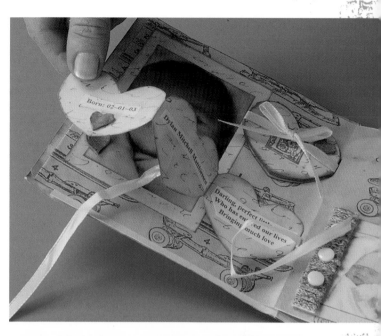

MATERIALS:
Design Originals Legacy Collage Papers (#0540 Skates and #0549 Shorthand) • Parchment cardstock • White copy paper • Black and white photocopies • Rubber stamps (*All Night Media* Ornamental Letters & Numbers) • *Clearsnap* Ancient Page Sienna ink pad • *Opaque* shrink plastic • *Krylon* 18 kt Metallic Gold Leafing Pen • 2 yards Ivory 1/4" ribbon • Double-stick tape.• Computer generated text • Heat gun

INSTRUCTIONS: Cut a 3 1/4" x 4 1/2" piece of Shorthand paper to mat the baby photo. Scale the photo to fit the mat. Stamp the name onto the pages of one heart booklet using Sienna ink. Computer print with Brown ink, name, date of birth, thoughts and deco theme. Tear or cut around the computer printing. Mount printing on the second accordion heart. Rub Sienna ink directly from ink pad onto all paper edges. Glue the center of an 18" ribbon to the center backs of the heart booklets. Use glue stick to adhere paper layers in place. Tie ribbons in bows. To make the small Gold hearts, color with metallic pens on shrink plastic. Cut out three 1 1/2" hearts. Shrink with a heat gun, then glue to the page with White glue. Glue heart button to front cover.

1. Cut a 2 1/2" wide strip of paper. Trace heart shape pattern on one end of the strip.

2. Fan-fold the paper so it is the width of the heart.

3. Cut out the heart shape leaving sections on one side uncut.

Bundle of Love Page

by Chris Malone

Show off your embroidery skills with this stitched heart.

MATERIALS:
Watercolor paper • *Contessa* Sahara rayon/silk • *Avanti* Variegated Rosedust rayon/cotton slub • Vintage buttons (2 Blue, 3 White) • Rubber stamps (*Uptown Design* #13148 Sweet Bundle) • Brown ink • Small copy of baby photo • Speckled Tan cardstock • Scrap vintage lace • Embroidery needle • Glue

INSTRUCTIONS:
Tear watercolor paper into a 3" x 3 1/2" rectangle. Lightly draw a heart in the center with a pencil. • Start at the center and satin stitch the heart with Contessa yarn. Sew a blue button to the center of heart with yarn. Tie the ends on top of the button and clip. • Mat the photo with Tan cardstock. • Cut a 1/2" x 2 3/4" strip from the watercolor paper. Wrap variegated yarn around the strip to cover completely. Tape or glue the ends of the yarn to the back of the strip. Glue the strip in place. Glue white buttons on the strip. • Tear a 2" x 1 3/4" rectangle from cardstock. Stamp a saying with Brown ink. Apply Brown ink with fingers or sponge applicator to the edges of all the rectangles. Glue pieces in place with lace and large button.

1. Make the hats and store in the pocket.

2. You can now change the baby hats.

Many Hats for Dylan - Left Page

by Dorothy Egan

Dream of the many possible futures for your children. Represent those dreams with several hats.

MATERIALS:
Design Originals Legacy Collage paper (#0540 Skates, #0544 Bingo) • Stamp pads (Light Green, Dark Green, Gold) • Vintage poetry • 1¹/₂" diameter photograph of baby • 2¹/₄" x 3¹/₂" manila envelope • Angel art • *Peel n Stick* • Words clipped from newspaper • Gold leafing pen • Restickable glue stick • 4 small brads • Vintage lace • Spray adhesive • Black permanent ink pad • Frog charm • Gold foil • Blue handmade paper • Red star print fabric • Newspaper clipping • Crimper

INSTRUCTIONS:
Sponge Light Green ink onto vintage poetry page. Repeat with Dark Green and touches of Gold ink. Tear paper to fit page. Attach to page with spray adhesive. • Glue a strip of old lace across the lower corner of the page. • Cut out the Bingo card. Cut an opening in the card to fit the photo. Glue the photo behind the opening. • Glue the Bingo card to the front of a manila envelope. Trim away the exposed top of the envelope. Attach card and envelope to the page with glue and brads. • Glue the angel print to the page. Print or handwrite quote. Cut out the quote and edge with a gold leafing pen. Glue quote, words clipped from newspaper and frog in place.

HATS:
CROWN: Run Gold foil through a crimper in both directions. Glue foil to backing paper and cut out crown. • BALL CAP: Cut cap from blue paper. Draw seam lines with black pen. • NEWSPAPER HAT: Cut an 8-1/2" x 11" section of newsprint. Reduce it in a copier to 10% of its original size. Cut a newspaper hat from the reduced copy. FABRIC HAT: Bond red fabric to Peel n Stick. Cut out the pointed hat. • Cut tabs from cardstock and glue to the back of each hat. Cut a slit in the photo to fit the tabs. Attach hats to the page with re-stickable glue or place in the envelope behind the Bingo card.

TIP: Make whatever hats are appropriate for your project.

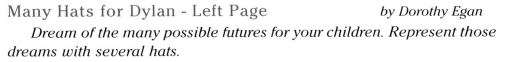

Accordion Book

This handy book is a great way to show off a grandbaby!

Welcome Dylan!
Right Page with Heart

by Beth Wheeler

Every culture has traditions welcoming a newborn into the community. This page captures the spirit of those wonderful traditions.

MATERIALS:
Design Originals Legacy Collage Paper (#0540 Skates) • Printout of favorite lullaby • Clear packing tape • Photocopy of favorite photo • Small square of cardstock • Artwork of a guardian angel, Cardstock • Clear embossing ink pad and powder • Gold embossing powder • Heat tool • Fibers • Small charms • Hammerhead Omni Stick clear gel adhesive

INSTRUCTIONS:
Cut a piece of Legacy Collage paper the size of the base page. Glue in place. • Tear the lullaby words slightly smaller than the background page. Glue in place.

Mount the baby photo on cardstock and glue in place. • Make a tape transfer with the words "Welcome Dylan" and adhere to page (see page 50). • Glue the guardian angel to a piece of cardstock. Cut it into a heart shape.

Apply clear embossing ink. Sprinkle with clear embossing powder. Heat with heat tool. • Repeat for a thick coating. In the last layer, sprinkle grains of gold embossing powder around the edges of the heart while clear is still molten. Allow to cool. • Place remaining items on the page. Secure with acid-free gel adhesive.

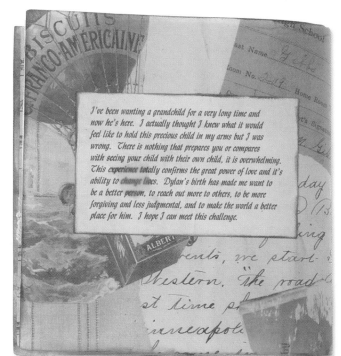

Back Cover

by Barbara Matthiessen

Write a letter to your grandchild or record your feelings for your grandchildren. Make a memory book for each grandbaby.

MATERIALS:
Design Originals Legacy Collage (#0538 Peter's Dreams) • White cardstock • *Ancient Page* Sienna ink pad • Computer generated font

INSTRUCTIONS:
Print a message in Brown ink. Tear or cut out the message. • Tint the edges of the paper with the Sienna ink pad. Glue the message to the collage paper.

All Through the Night

by Beth Wheeler

We all have our very favorite lullaby. Print yours and save it on this page.

MATERIALS:
Printout of lullaby on White paper

INSTRUCTIONS:
Print out your favorite lullaby and glue it to the deco page. Use any remaining space to write a message. Have fun!

Bingo Page

by Dorothy Egan

Handmade papers give texture to a collage reminiscent of the games we played as children. Celebrating a first grandchild makes everyone feel like a winner.

MATERIALS:
Design Originals Legacy Collage Paper (#0544 Bingo) • Handmade paper (Tan, Lacy White) • Tan cardstock • Parchment with printed message • Large button • Heavy thread • Printed game tiles

INSTRUCTIONS:
Glue the Tan cardstock to the page. Glue the Bingo card and scrap of White handmade paper in place. Run a thread through the buttonholes and tie a bow. Tear the edges of the parchment message. Glue the button, printed message and game tiles to the page.

Baby Hands Page

by Chris Malone

Every parent appreciates the ink print of their infant's hands and feet. Use the hand stamp to impart those emotions on this page.

MATERIALS:
Design Originals Legacy Collage Paper (#0549 Shorthand) • Dyed silk ribbon • *All Night Media* Baby Hands rubber stamp • Brown and Gray ink • Tan cardstock • Computer generated text

INSTRUCTIONS:
Print a message on the cardstock. Trim to fit page and ink edges. • Stamp baby hands with Gray ink. • Mount the cardstock on Shorthand paper and glue to the deco page. Tie a ribbon bow, glue in place.

In the Garden

by Chris Malone

This is the perfect project for anyone who loves gardening. Gather all the ephemera that brings you the peace and tranquility of a garden - charms of leaves, insects, flowers and birds. Enjoy creating something beautiful!

How to Make the Garden Book

MATERIALS:
Design Originals Legacy Collage Paper (#0528 Watches) • Two 4³/4" x 6¹/2" pieces of chipboard or mat board • Watercolor paper • Green leaf paper • Cream cardstock • Handmade paper scraps (Cream, Green) • Rubber stamps (*Magenta* Leaf; *PSX* Alphabet Pixies, Antique Lowercase; *The Stamping Ground*, Moon face; *Uptown Design* #103677 Little Tree) • Inks (Black, Green, Rose, Blue, Sienna) • 4 eyelets • Small brad • *Bucilla* 100% Pure Silk Ribbon (13 mm Terracotta variegated, 7 mm Burgundy) • 5 Green glass leaves • Garden theme charms • Assorted buttons including large metal shank button for closure • Green size 5 Pearl cotton • Seed beads (Green, Gold) • Scrap metallic Gold foil • Watch parts (³/4" – ⁷/8") • Wire-edged ribbon (12" piece Dark Rose Ombre, 5" piece Green Ombre) • Print of angels • *Krylon* 18kt. Gold Leafing Pen • Assorted fibers • 14" piece of Gold elastic cord • Assorted glass beads • Needles (embroidery, hand sewing, beading) • Pink thread or floss • Beading thread • Stylus • Sponge applicator • Glue • Computer generated font • Zig zag decorative edge scissors.

1. Wind the fibers around fingers to form tassel.

2. Tie off the tassel.

3. Thread the same fiber strand through the button shank and secure.

Create a Garden when you get Spring Fever.

How to Make the Garden Book

INSTRUCTIONS:
Cover outside of front and back covers with leaf paper and inside of covers with Watches paper. Color eyelets with Krylon pen; let dry. Attach two eyelets to one side of each cover. • Tear a $4^{1}/2$" x $5^{1}/2$" rectangle from watercolor paper. Stamp the moon face with Black ink. Make 3 large and 2 small spider web roses with silk ribbon for hair (see page 37). Glue glass leaves around the flowers. Glue the water can charm above the head. Glue the shovel at the neck. Use a sponge applicator or fingers to apply Rose and Green inks lightly to the background. Add Rose to cheeks and Blue to eyes. Stamp "in the garden" as shown. Glue paper to the front of the cover.

ASSEMBLING THE BOOK:
To assemble the Deco, cut 4 pages from tan cardstock and punch holes to correspond with the eyelet placement on the covers. • Apply *Krylon* Gold to a metal shank button. Let dry. • Fold the Gold elastic cord in half and thread both ends through the button shank. Tie the ends in a knot so that a 5" loop remains. Apply a dot of glue to the knot and trim the ends close to the knot. • To make a fiber tassel, cut assorted fibers into 16" lengths. Wrap the fibers around 4 fingers (about 4") two times and tie at the top with a different fiber. Tie again about $1/2$" down. Thread the same fiber strand through the button shank and secure. Tie garden tool charms to two fibers and add glass beads to another strand.

Inside Front Cover

Print "Time Began in a Garden" on cardstock • Tear the edges. • Apply Sienna ink to the edges. • Stamp tree onto Cream handmade paper with Sienna. Attach a leaf charm to the watch face with a brad. Arrange papers, angel print, watch face, and assorted buttons and glue them to the inside of the front cover.

Rabbit in my Garden

by Chris Malone

A twig and dried flowers combine with animal and insect charms to create this lovely scene.

MATERIALS:
Watercolor paper • Scraps of handmade & mulberry papers (Brown, Green) • *Contessa* rayon/silk blend yarns (Sahara, Copper, Scarlet) • Pressed flowers • Small twig • Rhodonite chips with holes • Scrap of Ivory organza • Charms (rabbit, dragonfly) • Vintage green trim • Button • Tape • Needles (embroidery, handsewing) • Ecru sewing thread • Glue

INSTRUCTIONS:
Tear the watercolor paper to fit the inside page. • Make guide lines for stitching the Sahara, Copper, and Scarlet threads. Lightly mark $1^{1}/4$" long pencil lines down the right side of the paper so there are $3/4$", 1" and $1^{1}/8$" spaces between the lines. • Satin stitch the top section with Sahara, center with Copper and bottom with Scarlet. Place the twig over the stitched area and couch into place by making small stitches over the twig. Sew rhodonite chips to form a flower shape and a few at side of the twig for leaves. • Glue the flowers to a torn scrap of brown paper. Place organza over the flowers and make random "x" stitches around the flowers with sewing thread. • Arrange and glue the green mulberry paper, flower piece, charms, trim and button in place. • Glue the paper to the page.

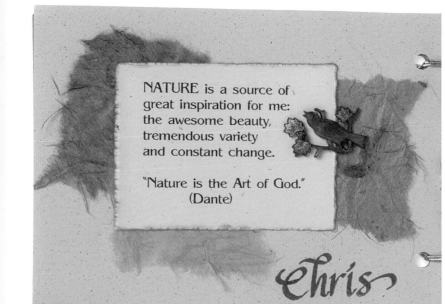

Nature is the Art of God

by Chris Malone

Express your favorite garden sentiment on this simple page.

MATERIALS:
Watercolor paper • Scraps of handmade & mulberry papers (Brown, Green) • Computer generated script • Brown chalk • Bird charm

INSTRUCTIONS:
Use three scraps of handmade or mulberry paper and glue in place as shown. • Print your sentiment on watercolor paper. Tear the edges. Chalk the edges with Brown. • Glue the script and the bird charm in place. • Sign your name.

Spring Time

by Dorothy Egan

Capture a moment in time with a vintage clock face and watch parts.

MATERIALS:
Spray adhesive • *X-acto* knife • Paintbrush • *Plaid* FolkArt acrylic paints (Dark Gray, Mushroom, Clover, Bayberry) • Handmade paper (Brown, Blue and Lacy White) • Large leaf • Vintage $2^1/2$" clock face • Micro beads (Gold, Green) • Dragonfly charm • Miniature Christmas garland • Clock gears • *Glass, Metal and More* Adhesive • *Plaid* Dimensional Magic • Green embroidery thread

TIP: To dry a leaf rapidly, place the leaf between layers of muslin and press with a warm iron.

INSTRUCTIONS:
Spray the back of Blue handmade paper with spray adhesive and attach to the page. Repeat with the white paper. • Cut a tree from the brown handmade paper. Use a small brush to pull Dark Gray and Mushroom from the edges toward the center on the tree truck to create a birch-bark appearance. Glue the tree near the outside edge of the page. • Use a dried leaf to frame the clock face. Cut a circle in the leaf to fit the clock face. Glue leaf to clock face. Glue leaf and clock to background page. • Glue garland greenery at the base of the tree. Use embroidery floss for flower stems. Glue stems and gear 'flowers' in place above the greenery. • Squeeze Dimensional Magic along branches in random shapes to suggest leaf clusters. Drop micro beads into the glue. Let dry, then shake to remove excess beads. Glue the dragonfly in place.

Make a Cheerful Garden Book

Sun & Moon Signature Page

by Dorothy Egan

Find your favorite charm or decoration to show off your signature.

MATERIALS:
Plaid FolkArt acrylic paints (Sterling Blue, Bayberry) • *Fresco* Giovani's Garden ink pad • Green handmade paper • Sun charm • 3 ribbon rosebuds • Clock face stamp

INSTRUCTIONS:
Lightly paint fern-like leaves with Sterling Blue, then with Bayberry. • Stamp over the leaves with clock face stamp. • Tear a rectangle of green paper and glue on the page. Sign and date the page. Glue the sun charm and ribbon roses to the page.

Inside Back Cover

A large rose shaped with wire-edged ribbon and a leaf merge with timely charms to express a word of thanks.

Write a Thank You message and print it onto cardstock. Tear the edge, add ink and glue to the inside of the back cover.

RIBBON ROSE: See page 29. To make ribbon rose, tie a knot at one end of Rose ribbon. Pull one wire to tightly gather one side of the ribbon. Roll ribbon around knot, then in looser rounds until rose shape is formed. Wrap the wire around the knot to secure and trim the excess. Use fingers to shape and press down on rose. To make ribbon leaf, fold a Green ribbon in half so the halves lay side by side. Pull the center wire from both ends to gather, and twist the wires together to secure. Glue message, watch parts and ribbon rose with leaf to the inside of the back cover.

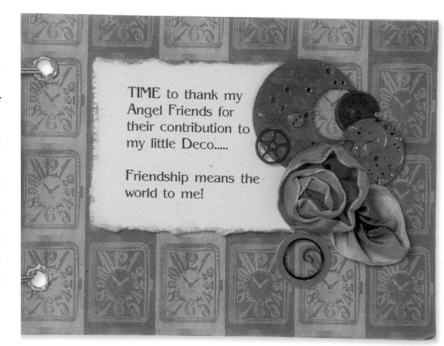

Stitch Diagrams

by Chris Malone

When stitching on paper, it is helpful to use the needle to first make a hole on the front where the needle will come up from the back.

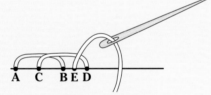

Stem Stitch

Bring the needle up at A. Insert the needle at B and bring it up at C, about halfway between A and B. Pull the thread through and go back in at D, coming up at E. Repeat pattern to complete.

Satin Stitch

Bring the needle up at A, down at B, forming a smooth straight stitch. Bring the needle up again at C, down at D, forming another straight stitch that lies close to the first. Repeat the pattern until covered. • It is important to make the long stitch on the back to stabilize the stitching holes. Beginning and ending yarns can be held in place on the back with a dot of glue or small piece of tape. If stitching holes do tear, use a piece of tape on the back to hold the yarn in place.

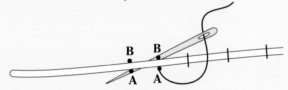

Couching Stitch

Bring the needle up at A; pass over yarn or subject to be attached (wire, twig, etc.) and go down at B. Repeat as necessary to attach item securely and evenly.

Spider Web Rose

Draw a circle with a pencil somewhat smaller than the completed rose will be. Put a dot at the center and at five equally spaced sections of the circle. • Thread a needle with doubled floss or thread and make a stitch from each outer dot to the center dot, keeping spokes taut. • Thread ribbon in a needle and bring it up at the center, close to the floss. Stay on the surface of the fabric and weave the ribbon over and under the spokes, alternating as the ribbon goes round and round. Keep the ribbon even but not too tight and let it softly twist for better petals. When full and complete, insert the needle though to the back of fabric.

TIP: Use the blunt end of the needle to weave through the stitches.

Draw a circle somewhat smaller than the finished rose size. Space dots in center and evenly around the circle.	Stitch with floss or thread from each outer dot to the center dot, keeping spokes taut.	Bring ribbon up at center, close to the floss. Stay on the surface of the fabric, weave ribbon over and under spokes, alternating as ribbon goes round.

Choose your favorite season, animal, flower, or quote to make a Garden Book.

Garden Flowers

by Beth Wheeler

Dimensional flowers and bright colors bring a touch of summer to this page.

MATERIALS:
Scrap of multi-colored floral fabric • Butterfly ephemera • White polymer clay • Floral rubber stamp • Various mica-based eye shadows • Toothpick • Household oven • Baking sheet • Baking parchment • Flower-shape clay cutter • Adhesive • Garden quote printed on glossy White paper • Clear packing tape • Bone folder • 26-gauge wire • Assorted small beads • Wire cutter • Needle-nose pliers • *Krylon (14K Gold leaf pen, spray acrylic sealer)*
TIP: If the print is so bold you have trouble finding the butterflies, use the wrong side of the fabric.

INSTRUCTIONS:

Cut a piece of fabric slightly smaller than the deco page. Fringe the edges slightly. • Outline the page with Gold leaf pen and glue the fabric on the page. • Roll the polymer clay to an even thickness. Stamp multiple times with rubber stamp for texture. • Cut the flowers out with the clay cutter and poke a hole in the center with a toothpick. • Rub eye shadow into the clay with your finger. Gently bend the petals into a cup shape. • Place flowers on a baking sheet lined with baking parchment. Bake according to instructions on the package. • Cool. Spray with acrylic sealer. Let dry. • Cut one short piece of wire for each blossom. Coil one end. Insert the straight end of one wire piece through one blossom from back to front (the coil will prevent it from slipping out). • Put one or two small beads on the straight end of the wire and twist and curl the wire into an interesting shape. Cut the excess off with wire cutters. Repeat with remaining wire and blossoms. • Prepare the message as a tape transfer (see page 50). Glue clay blossoms, butterfly ephemera and message in a pleasing arrangement on the deco page.

LOVE Notes from the Garden

Garden Love Notes

by Beth Wheeler

Write a note about your love for gardening and store it in a decorative pocket.

MATERIALS:
Library book pocket or similar envelope • Rubber stamp and ink pad in desired color • Small piece of scrapbook paper • *Krylon* 14k Gold Leaf pen

INSTRUCTIONS:
Write a message on the unprinted side of the scrapbook paper and fold it to fit inside the library pocket. Outline the note with Gold-leaf pen. • Stamp the background page and library pocket. Outline both with Gold leaf pen. • Glue the library pocket on the deco page. Insert your message into the library pocket. Sign and date the pocket with the Gold leaf pen.

Joy in the Garden
by Lynda Musante

Express your favorite garden sentiment on this simple page.

MATERIALS:
Design Originals Legacy Papers (#0547 Dictionary) • *Fiskars* Deckle Paper Edgers • *Making Memories* Eyelet Alphabet • *Rubber Stampede* Fern stamp • "In the Garden" word stamp or desired phrase • Pigment ink (Green, Black) • Dye ink (Light Green, Dark Green) • Clear *Ultra Thick Embossing Enamel* (UTEE) • Black embossing powder • Ivory cardstock • *USArtquest* (Matte Perfect Paper Adhesive (PPA); Perfect FX Mica Tiles) • *Glue Dots:* Pop-up Dots • *Halcraft USA Inc.* $1/2$" wide Curiously Sticky Tape • Heat gun • Tweezers • $1/8$" punch • Eyelet setting tool • Hammer • Several stipple brushes • Brayer

INSTRUCTIONS:
Cut cardstock $1/8$" smaller than page size with deckle scissors. • Use stipple brushes to pounce drifts of Light Green around the edges of the cardstock, concentrating color at the outer edge. Sparingly pounce Dark Green around the outer edge. • Use Dark Green ink to stamp fern image on 3 mica tiles. Sprinkle with UTEE and melt with a heat gun. • Stamp word phrase in Black ink on Dictionary paper. • Sprinkle with Black embossing powder and melt with a heat gun. • Arrange the stamped mica tiles and stamped phrase on the page, leaving space for the eyelet letters. Adhere items with PPA. • Cover with scrap paper and burnish with a brayer. • Arrange eyelet letters as desired and press down firmly, indenting the paper. Use a $1/8$" punch to make holes and attach the eyelets.

Back Cover:
by Chris Malone

Stamp a leaf on watercolor paper with green ink. • Use a doubled length of beading thread and a beading needle to sew Green and Gold seed beads to the center vein of the leaf. Pick up three beads on a needle, poke into paper and come up between first and second bead; go back through the last two beads and pick up three more.

Repeat this pattern until complete. Satin stitch some sections of leaf with pearl cotton. Cut out leaf $1/4$" from outline. • Use zig zag scissors to cut metal foil into rough leaf shape. Use a stylus to draw tiny swirls all over the foil on one side which will be the back of the leaf. Glue the foil, beaded leaf and bug charm to the cover.

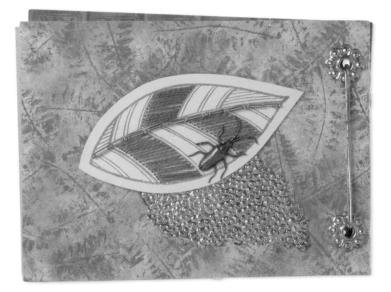

My Garden in Autumn
by Lynda Musante

This page captures the spirit of Fall in lovely copper tones.

MATERIALS:
Ivory cardstock • Leaf rubber stamps • Dye ink (Brown, Beige, Gray) • Computer printed garden quote • *USArtquest* (Matte Perfect Paper Adhesive PPA • *USArtquest* Perfect FX Mica Tiles • Metal bee charm • *Glue Dots:* Pop-up Dots • *Fiskars* Deckle Paper Edgers • *Halcraft* $1/2$" wide Curiously Sticky tape • Heat gun • Tweezers • Stipple brushes • Brayer

INSTRUCTIONS:
Stamp Brown leaf images on cardstock repeating each image without re-inking the stamp • Use a stipple brush to lightly pounce Beige ink across the page, softening the stamped images. Lightly pounce Gray ink around the edges of the page. • Separate mica tiles into thin pieces. Arrange tiles in a pleasing manner and adhere with PPA. • Attach garden quote with PPA. Attach metal bee charm with two pop-up Glue Dots. • Adhere card front and card back to the page using strips of Curiously Sticky tape.

Purse Book

by Billie Worrell

Clean all the memorabilia out of your purse, and give it an attractive, permanent home.

How to Make the Purse

MATERIALS:
Design Originals Legacy Collage Papers (#0536 Violets Hanky, #0551 Legacy Words) • *SEI* Eggplant Velvet Paper • Vellum (Blue, White) • Cardstock (Lavender, Red) • *Delta* Sobo Glue • *Making Memories* Details 1/8" Metallic Brass Eyelets • *Clorox* Ultra Advantage Bleach • Computer printed images and photos • *Rubber Stampede* (Pigment Ink Pads: Purple, Chocolate, Turquoise, Fuchsia; Wood Handle Stamps: #All02E Monkey Paw Fern, #3343F Memories, #3322R Music Background and #A860E Elegant "LOVE"; Fun Type Alphabet Stamp Set; School Days Stamp Kit) • *Delta* (Brown Antiquing Gel, acrylic paint) • Violet *Perfect Pearls* • *Creative Imaginations* Faux Wax Seals • Metal tag • *DMD* (Shipping Tags, Butterflies, Vellum die-cuts) • Vellum envelope • Vellum tape • Miscellaneous fibers • Key ring • 24mm purple button • 7" *Create A Craft* 1 mm Natural Leather Cord • 1 yard Gold metallic 4mm cord • Velcro

Inside of Purse Cover

Show off your pictures, souvenirs and memorabilia on the inside of your purse book.

Page Pattern

How to Make the Purse

To make the clasp on the outside, center and glue a button on the top flap. • To make the purse handle, run metallic cord through the buttonholes and knot on the inside. • Punch two holes side by side in the center of the inside flap and 1" from top edge. • Paint the natural leather cord with Violet Pearls paint to match the cover and let dry. Thread the cord through the holes from the inside.

Glue an image or piece of paper to cover. Tie the purple cords in a knot to complete the purse fastener. • Place an eyelet 1/8" from the left edge of purse directly under the top fold. • Place an eyelet in the upper left corner of each page. Attach the pages to the purse with key ring. • Decorate the inside of the purse cover with scanned images and torn pieces of collage paper. Tint the edges of the paper with Purple ink. Use the alphabet stamp set and household bleach to stamp "My Dolls" onto the page. • A vellum envelope contains butterflies signed by each designer. To make the envelope, cut the flap of the envelope off. Sponge Turquoise, Fuchsia and Purple ink and let dry.

• Stamp music background onto the vellum with bleach. • Insert die-cut butterflies into the envelope. Glue one butterfly to the outside of the envelope. Attach the envelope to the bottom of the inside cover with vellum tape.

Purse Cover Pattern
Score and fold along dashed lines.
Circles indicate eyelet placement.

How to Make the Purse Cover

MATERIALS:
Computer, scanner and printer • No. 10 shader paintbrush • *Making Memories* Details Eyelet Tool • Stylus or scoring tool • 1/8" hole punch • Silk sponge

INSTRUCTIONS:
Place the purse pattern on Lavender paper and page pattern on the white. Trace with pencil and cut out. • Glue Lavender cutout of purse to the back of the Eggplant velvet paper using Sobo glue. Let dry and trim. • Reposition the pattern on the Lavender side. Score along the lines. • Place the ruler on the lines and fold, giving shape to the purse. • Add a small piece of Velcro under the flap and on front to fasten. • Place a paper towel on a plastic plate and pour bleach onto it. Wet the stamp with bleach and stamp on the velvet paper at random. • Tear around image copies. Stamp the edges with ink by holding the pad at an angle.

1. Glue Lavender paper to back side of velvet paper.

2. Trim velvet paper to size.

3. Position paper pattern on Lavender paper. Use the pattern to score fold lines.

4. Stamp onto velvet side of purse with bleach.

Memories in my Purse Book

Love is Forever
by Tracia Williams

We carry pictures of loved ones in our purses to keep them close. This attractive page provides a space for our photos and all the little beads we collect.

MATERIALS:
Beige cardstock • Assorted vintage images • *Plaid* Dimensional Magic • *All Night Media* Anna Griffin (Hydrangea Stamp, Background Stamp) • *Ranger* Archival Ink Pads (Grape, Coffee) • *Sulyn Industries* (Assorted beads, letter beads and micro beads) • 22 gauge wire • *Loew Cornell* Watercolors • #3 round brush

INSTRUCTIONS:
Cut 2 page shapes from Beige cardstock and glue them together to.make the page front and back. • Punch a hole and set an eyelet in the corner as shown in the photo. • Use Coffee ink to stamp the background. Stamp the hydrangea using Grape ink on the Coffee background. Softly color the hydrangea using watercolors and #3 brush. Let dry. • Glue the photo next to the hydrangea image. • Trace the photo edge with Dimensional Magic. Add beads and the word "LOVE". • Using a 10" piece of wire, curl the end, add beads and word "IS FOREVER". Curl other end of wire. • Position the words on wire over the Dimensional Magic. Sprinkle with micro beads. Let dry. Shake off excess.

Decorate Every Page in a New Way.

Angel Page
by Tracia Williams

Angels are everywhere. Keep your guardian close on this page.

MATERIALS:
Beige cardstock • Vintage angel image • *All Night Media* Anna Griffin Background Stamp • *Ranger* Grape Archival ink pad

INSTRUCTIONS:
This is the back of the Love Is Forever page. Stamp the background using Grape ink. Glue the angel image in place. Write a message.

It's All About a Girl
by Kim Ballor

The green edge of a handkerchief forms the leaves while the folds and beads suggest a rose on this creative page

MATERIALS:
Old handkerchief • Size 11 seed beads to match • Beading needle • Beading thread • Assorted charms, beads, and found ephemera • Computer printed words: "It's all about a girl" • Purple pages torn from a magazine

INSTRUCTIONS:
Cut a magazine page the same size as the deco page. • Cut a piece of handkerchief to fit page. Fold and pleat the handkerchief. Lightly glue it to the magazine paper to hold it while you stitch. • Backstitch seed beads around the pattern to hold the handkerchief to the paper. • Cut words apart. Stitch seed beads at the corners of the words to hold them in place. • Use beads, charms, and found ephemera to make dangles. Stitch to the top right corner of paper. • Glue paper to the deco page.

1. Heat the foam with a heat gun.

2. Press a stamp onto warm foam.

Medallion Compact
by Barbara Matthiessen

A compact medallion holds accordion photos instead of make-up. The compact is made from craft foam.

MATERIALS:
Design Originals Legacy Collage Papers (#0534 Ruth's Violets, #0536 Violets Hanky) • *All Night Media* Anna Griffin rubber stamps (Bow Motif, Georgian Cartouche, Rose Background, Browning Poem) • Lavender Chalk ink pad • *Tsukineko* VersaMagic Pretty Petunia • *Plaid* Treasure Gold • 12" heavy lace • 4" x 8" sheet white craft foam • 2 jewelry pieces • Heat gun

INSTRUCTIONS:
Stamp Rose Background and Bow Motif onto the page using Lavender ink. • Trim a violet cluster from Violets Hanky paper and glue to the deco page.

MAKE THE COMPACT:
Heat the craft foam with a heat gun until a slight sheen appears on the surface. • Immediately press the stamp down onto warm foam. Press down with full body weight for 15 seconds. Repeat on compact back. • Trim around the embossed image leaving a small tab for the front cover. • Rub metallic finish over the foam surfaces.

ASSEMBLE THE COMPACT:
Glue lace to the back of the compact. • Accordion fold Violets Hanky paper to fit inside compact. Round off the corners. • Stamp Browning Poem on yellow area of Violets Hanky paper and tear to fit compact. Tear photos from Ruth's Violets paper to fit compact. • Glue torn poem and photos to pages in accordion book. Glue the last page of the accordion book to the center of compact back. Glue compact front tab to the page. Glue jewelry to the compact.

Make Tags & Tassels
by Billie Worrell

Make a whimsical key ring tassel in matching colors.

Sponge one tag with Fuchsia and Purple inks and the other with Purple and Turquoise inks. • Using the Memories stamp and bleach, stamp onto Lavender cardstock. Tear out and glue onto the Purple/Turquoise tag. • Cut the tag so it will be smaller than the other. • Glue an image to the Fuchsia/Purple tag. Glue a small photo to the other tag. Connect these to the keyring with fibers.

Purple Necklace on a Page
by Barbara Matthiessen

Next time you clean out your purse, save that broken necklace for this pretty deco page.

MATERIALS:
Design Originals Legacy Collage Paper (#0534 Ruth's Violets) • *All Night Media* Anna Griffin rubber stamps (Bow Motif, Rose Background) • Lavender chalk ink pad • Pendant jewelry piece • 8" Lavender 3mm ribbon

INSTRUCTIONS:
Stamp the Rose Background and Bow Motif onto the page using Lavender ink. • Trim a violet cluster, photo, and label from Ruth's Violets paper. • Layer and glue to deco page using glue stick. • Tie a ribbon through the pendant. Glue the pendant and ribbon to the page with White glue.

Pockets Book

by Kim Ballor

The great part about making pages out of pockets is that you can have tags and found objects peeking out. When making this book, each artist used a monochromatic scheme based on the color of her choice.

Have fun experimenting with colors and themes of your own.

How to Make the Book

TIP: Photocopy the eyeglasses before wiring them to the book.

MATERIALS:
Clear plastic folder for cover • Color pages torn from magazines • *All Night Media* (Jive Alphabet set, Swirl Pattern Stamp) • *Cat's Life Press* ART stamp • Rainbow ink pad • 14 square Silver eyelets • 46 small round Brass eyelets and setting tools • Silver and Green craft wire • Wire cutters • 2-3 large glass beads • Nine 4mm Green crystal glass beads • Pair of old glasses • 4 library pockets • Double-stick tape • Assorted buttons, postage stamps, etc • 1/8" hole punch • *Plaid* Dimensional Magic • Fibers and yarns • Charms and beads • Size 11 seed beads • Posterboard

MAKING THE BOOK:
Cut two same size rectangles, a little larger than the size of your library pockets, from the clear folder. • Set 7 square eyelets (evenly aligned) up one side of each plastic rectangle. These form the front and back covers of the book. • Set 7 round eyelets up the left side of each library pocket. Measure and mark where to set each eyelet, so they line up when you wire the pages together. • Cut 36" of craft wire. After decorating each page, loop the wire through the eyelets and hold the 4 pockets and the front and back page together. Twist the wire around itself and trim at each end.

MAKING THE COVER:
Tear and glue pieces of magazine pages and tape them to the cover, leaving a section on the right side blank. On a light color paper, stamp the words "the eyes have it". Tear the words apart and tape in place. Stamp any additional words or messages you like on the cover. • Cut 36" of wire to tie the eyeglass stems together, then wire the glasses to the spiral that is holding the deco together. • Punch a hole at the center bottom of the cover. Make a small loop in one end of 6" of wire. Slide 3 beads onto the wire. Slide the free end of the wire through the hole in the cover and wrap the wire around itself to secure the dangle to the cover.

Pocket Page
by Kim Ballor

MATERIALS:
Magazine clippings • Rubber stamps and stamp pads • 18 round eyelets • 18" of Green craft wire • Crystal beads • *Royal Coat* Dimensional Magic • 3" x 6" posterboard • Seed beads • Fibers and yarn • Assorted charms

INSIDE THE COVER:
Tape magazine pages to the inside front cover, leaving the same area blank. Stamp images as desired. Glue ephemera in place.

FIRST PAGE:
Tape or glue torn magazine pages and images to cover the library pocket. Stamp images as desired. • Set 9 pairs of round eyelets running up the right side of the pocket from the bottom. • Cut 18" of Green craft wire. Wire Crystal beads between each pair of eyelets. • Twist the wire around itself on the back to secure and trim the end. Cover the back with decorative paper and write a note.

MAKING THE TAG:
Photocopy the pair of glasses you used on the front cover Glue the photocopy to posterboard and cut out. • Squeeze Dimensional Magic onto the cutout and sprinkle with seed beads. Let dry. • Punch a hole at one end of glasses. Thread fibers and yarn through the hole. Tie charms and beads to the ends of the fibers.

Look... See
by Chris Malone

Oh what you can do...let your imagination run free.

MATERIALS:
Watercolor paper • Blue cardstock • Paper scraps (Cream, Dark Blue, Blue vellum) • 2 shades blue ink • *DMC* Blue rayon floss • 7" of 24 gauge Gold wire • Blue glass seed beads • 10" of Blue mesh ribbon • 2" x 1¹/2" oval mirror • 15" of 22 gauge Silver wire • Silver button • Large Silver eyelet • *All Night Media* Jive Alphabet Rubber Stamp Set • Old mirror tool (jewelry repair or dentist tool) • Blues poetry dog tag • Beading thread • Embroidery needle • Tape • Toothpick • Sponge applicator

INSTRUCTIONS:
Cover the front of the envelope, including the top section of the back with cardstock. Tear the watercolor paper to fit on the pocket. • Apply Blue inks to the paper with sponge applicators or fingers. • Thread beads onto Gold wire until a 5" section is beaded. Curl the ends by tightly wrapping the ends around a toothpick. • Shape into an "S" with fingers and place on inked paper. Couch wire to card by making small stitches across the wire between the beads every ¹/2" using beading thread.

Draw "e's" with a pencil and stem stitch over the lines with three strands of floss. Glue paper to the front of the envelope. • Cut

a 2" piece from ribbon and glue ribbon and mirror to the bottom of the paper. Cut a 6" piece from Silver wire and thread it through two holes of a Silver button. Curl the ends of the wire and glue the button to the paper.

MAKING THE TAG:
Cut a 2¹/2" x 3¹/2" rectangle from cardstock. Round off the corners on one end. • Attach an eyelet to the top of the tag. • Stamp "LOOK" on a 2¹/2"x 1¹/2" piece of torn Cream paper. Layer "Look" over a small piece of blue vellum and glue in place.

Thread blue ribbon through the eyelet and tie a single knot. Place the stem of a mirror tool over the knot and knot again, tying the dental mirror in place • Push the remaining silver wire through the eyelet. Twist to hold. • Curl the wire and add a dog tag midway on one wire end. (If desired, whipstitch or glue wire to the ribbon at the back of the tag to stabilize.)

Pockets Book

Beaded Triangle
by Barbara Matthiessen

This book is made from a clear plastic folder and library pockets... all ready to hold your glasses.

MATERIALS:
Light Blue cardstock printed with computer fonts • *All Night Media* stamps (Ransom Alphabet, Swirl Border, Lace Doily Background) • Silver embossing powder • *ColorBox* stamp pad (Oyster White, Royal Blue) • *Plaid* Dimensional Magic • *Sulyn* Micro Beads (Silver, Blue) • Silver eyelets • Medium Blue handmade paper • Blue fibers • Magazine clipping of eyes • Heat gun

INSTRUCTIONS:
Make eye background paper by printing the word "eyes" on Blue cardstock in a variety of fonts in a Blue ink. • Cut 2 triangle accordion books using eye background. Stamp E,Y,E,S from alphabet stamp set using Oyster White ink. Emboss with Silver. • Glue bits of paper and magazine clipping in place. Fold triangles to make the accordion book. • Cut front and back covers from Blue cardstock slightly larger than triangle folds. Tear handmade paper triangles slightly larger than covers. • Stamp Royal Blue swirls. Glue magazine clipped eyes in place. Draw a line of Dimensional Magic around each eye. Sprinkle on Blue beads. Add a little more Dimensional Magic. Sprinkle on Silver beads. Allow to dry. • Glue 12" of fibers to back of each book then glue on the covers. • Place books side by side with top inside corners overlapping. Place an eyelet in the center joining both books and one on the left hand side. Tie fibers through the left eyelet. Slide one book into the pocket. Attach the other book to the tag.

TO MAKE THE POCKET:
Trim eye background paper slightly smaller than the pocket. • Stamp the lace background using Oyster White ink. Tear handmade paper slightly larger than the eye background. Glue in layers to the pocket. • Tear handmade paper to fit above the pocket. Glue in place. • Arrange magazine clipped eyes, glue a backing on the largest one with a piece of handmade paper. Glue in place.

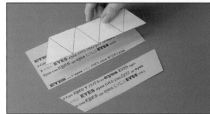

1. Trace triangle book pattern onto cardstock. Score on lines.

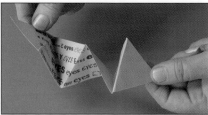

2. Fold into triangle shape.

3. Trace around folded book onto cover paper. Cut covers slightly larger.

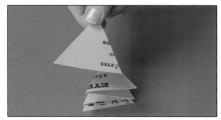

4. Glue covers on each end.

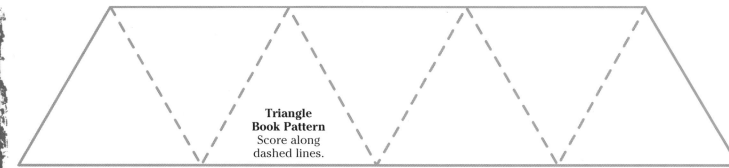

Triangle Book Pattern
Score along dashed lines.

Pockets are a great way to tuck in tags for special messages.

Five Foot Two, Eyes of Blue
by Chris Malone

Is there a song or poem about your eyes? Show it off on this page.

MATERIALS:
Blue cardstock • Blue mulberry paper • 2 shades Blue ink • Blue button • Dictionary clipping ("eye") • Magazine photo of doll face • Sponge applicator

INSTRUCTIONS:
Apply ink to color the envelope. Write a message on a small scrap of Blue cardstock. Arrange and glue the dictionary clipping, magazine picture, message and Blue button to the page.

Eyes on the World
by Dorothy Egan

Collect memorabilia that reflects your view of the universe.

MATERIALS:
Plaid FolkArt Metallic acrylic paints (Peridot, Silver Sterling, Inca Gold, Taupe) • Paper tag • Lacy White handmade paper • Vintage jewelry; • Scrap of rubber strip liner • Micro beads (Gold, Green) • Eye milagro charm • Eyeglass lens • Cutouts of eyes, world map and window • 1 1/2" Sheer and 3/4" satin ribbon • Fibers • Green vellum • Spray adhesive • X-acto knife • Paint brush • Drill with small bit • 2 brads

MAKING THE TAG:
Paint both sides of the tag with random strokes of metallic colors. • Punch out a design in the bottom of the tag. Paint the rubber strip liner scrap with Green and Gold and emboss after each ink application. Cut irregular narrow strips of finished liner. • Glue ribbons and rubber liner trim along the edges of the tag. • Turn the tag over. Layer the lacy White handmade paper and vellum with printed message. Glue in place. • Drill a hole in the eyeglass lens. Glue eye cutout to the back of the lens. Thread a Gold cord through the hole. Attach the lens, cord and fibers through the tag hole.

MAKING THE POCKET:
Paint the front of the library card holder with random strokes of metallic colors. Tear the world map to fit page. Cut away the pane of the window picture and glue eye behind the window. • Position and glue ribbon, map scrap, eye milagro charm, and eye window in place. • Use brads to attach a length from a vintage bracelet at the top of the pocket.

Back Side of Eyes on the World
by Dorothy Egan

Choose colors and embellishments to match your eyes when making this note page.

MATERIALS:
Handmade paper (Green and lacy White) • Music stamp • Light and Dark Green ink pads • Vintage button • Micro beads •*Plaid* Royal Coat Dimensional Magic • Foam pad or sponge

THE BACK OF THE POCKET:
Use a foam pad or sponge to lightly rub inks on the back of library pocket. Stamp music on green paper with dark green ink. Glue music and lacy paper to the pocket. Print the quote on green handmade paper. Tear to fit the page. Glue quote to the page. Use Dimensional Magic to attach micro beads at bottom of page. Glue button in place.

Tag Book

by Beth Wheeler

Capture the romance of travel in France. If you have always wanted to go to Paris, make this altered travel deco book from shipping tags using images from The Ephemera Book.

If you have been to France, this is the perfect place to display your memorabilia.

Ooh-la-la Paris! Cover
by Beth Wheeler

TIP: The cover background is an ad for a French airline. Other goodies include a map of France, old postcards, and a subway timetable. The subway timetable actually opens. It was printed on cardstock and folded like a tiny book. Write a secret message inside, if desired. Design Originals "The Ephemera Book" is a wonderful source for images of old posters, postcards, stamps, clip art, and other vintage memorabilia.

MATERIALS:
Design Originals Legacy Collage Paper (#0529 Le Jardin) • Shipping tag • Assorted French and Parisian vintage images • Packing tape transfer with desired words(see page 50 for directions) • *Hammerhead* Omni-Stick Acid-free gel adhesive.

INSTRUCTIONS:
Cut a piece of one paper for a background; glue to the tag with gel adhesive. • Layer remaining images, overlapping as desired. Allow any three-dimensional pieces, such as the subway timetable to be on the top.

Old Candy Containers
by Billie Worrell

Bleaching creates this interesting background on which to display your collection. Antique candy containers give sparkle to this page.

Use the Damask Flourish Decorative Stamp. Stamp onto bleach and stamp the Black gel paper at random. Cut out and glue shapes onto the tag. • Cut images of choice (I used French candy containers) and glue to tag. • Emboss around the edges of the tag with embossing ink and Gold embossing powder. • Use 1/4" paper hole punch to cut out the original hole in the tag.

Oui Paris

by Lynda Musante

Say YES! to Paris. This tag features art, people, places and symbols of the most beautiful city in France, the City of Lights.

MATERIALS:
Shipping tag • 5-6 Paris-themed images • *Making Memories* 1/8" Eyelet Alphabet • *ColorBox* (Pageant Petal Point Pigment Option Pad, Black, Blue and Silver Pigment Ink, Bisque Fluid Chalk Ink) • Black and Silver Embossing Powder • Clear Ultra Thick Embossing Enamel (UTEE) • Printed vellum • Fleur de lis rubber stamp • Clear embossing gel • Ivory cardstock • *Golden* Gel Medium (Extra Coarse Pumice Gel) • Black *Delta* Ceramcoat acrylic paint • Heat gun • Several stipple brushes • Brayer • Palette knife • Paper plate • Artist paintbrush • 1/8" punch • Eyelet setting tool • Hammer • 1/4" hole punch • Paper towel

TAG FRONT:
Cover work area. • Use stipple brushes to pounce drifts of color from Petal Point ink pads across the background. • Tear out an image and lightly brush the edges against a black ink pad. Dip inked edges into black embossing powder and tap off the excess. Melt embossing powder with a heat gun. • Following the outline closely, cut out an image with faces. Use a glue stick to adhere images to a shipping tag (see photo for placement). Cover with scrap paper and use a brayer to firmly burnish images onto the surface. • Lightly brush the edges of the tag against the Bisque Fluid Chalk ink pad to give the edges an aged look. • Cover the tag with a thin layer of embossing gel using a paintbrush. Pour UTEE over wet surface and tap off the excess. Melt with a heat gun. While UTEE is still quite hot, pour another layer of UTEE over the tag and tap off the excess. Melt with heat gun. Allow to cool. Use 1/8" punch to make holes and attach eyelets as shown.

Tag Back

Cover work area. • Use stipple brushes to pounce drifts of color from Petal Point ink pads across background. Use Blue ink to stamp Fleur de lis images randomly across tag. Use a glue stick to adhere images to the tag (see photo.) Cover the surface with scrap paper and use a brayer to firmly burnish images onto the surface. • Cut vellum to same size as tag, and use 1/4" hole punch to punch hole. • Lightly brush the edges of the vellum against silver ink pad and dip inked edges into silver embossing powder. Tap off the excess and melt with a heat gun. • The vellum is attached to the tag on one edge only. Use a glue stick to adhere vellum to the tag, aligning the edges. Cover with scrap paper and use brayer to firmly burnish images onto surface.

Tag Front

Using palette knife, thoroughly mix a small amount (quarter-sized) of Extra Coarse Pumice Gel with a dime-sized amount of black acrylic paint on a paper plate. Use a palette knife to transfer the Gel mixture to the tag to create a raised border around one image. Wipe the palette knife clean and use it to create straight edges on the border. Allow to dry completely.

A Day Trip to Paris

by Billie Worrell

Collect memorabilia to make this wonderful page.

MATERIALS:
Sepia vellum paper • Black gel paper • *Clorox* Ultra Advantage bleach • *Rubber Stampede* (Damask Flourish Decorator Stamp #73113, Embossing stamp pad) • Gold embossing powder • *Delta* Sobo glue • Images and photocopies • Charm and fibers • *Plaid* Royal Coat Dimensional Magic • Tiny glass marbles • Round silk sponge • 1/4" paper hole punch

INSTRUCTIONS:
Use the round silk sponge and sponge bleach onto the Sepia vellum paper at random. Glue the bleached paper to the tag and punch a hole over the original on the tag. • Reduce any copies of images and glue in place. (I used magazine images, photos, postal stamp and a card on the sample). • Squeeze Dimensional Magic directly from the bottle onto the edge of the tag. Cover with tiny marbles and let dry. • Add fibers to the Eiffel Tower charm and glue in place.

Bella Paris

by Tracia L. Williams

This tag presents beautiful women in Paris.

MATERIALS:
Design Originals Legacy Collage Paper (0529 Le Jardin) • Assorted charms, beads, tiny glass beads, and fibers • Alphabet stamp set • Copper ink pad • 3 small tags • Vintage piece of tape measure • *Krylon* Copper pen • Pop Dots

INSTRUCTIONS:
Cover page tag and small tag with Le Jardin paper. Outline the tags with a copper pen. • Add fibers to the small tag. Tie the fibers to the center ribbon of the deco. Use pop dots to attach the small tag. • Glue the tape measure in place. Glue charms and beads to tag referring to photo for placement. • Stamp words "Dame Bella" with rubber stamp and Copper ink.

Bien Venue

by Beth Wheeler

Enjoy making this project.

MATERIALS:
Design Originals Legacy Collage Paper (#0546 Currency) • Shipping tag • Assorted French and Parisian vintage images • Packing tape transfer with desired words and artwork • Candle • Matches • Clear acrylic spray sealant

INSTRUCTIONS:
Cut a piece of Currency paper the size of the shipping tag. Glue the paper to the tag. Trim the corners of paper to match the tag. • When the glue is dry, light the candle and burn the edges of the tag/background sandwich. Allow the carbon from the smoke to collect on the paper. • Wipe excess carbon from the paper, allowing some to remain. Spray with acrylic sealant to prevent it from rubbing off later. Let the sealant dry. • Layer the postcards, artwork and tape transfers on the background. Secure with glue.

MAKE A PACKING TAPE TRANSFER

MATERIALS:
Clear packing tape (the wider the tape, the larger the image you can transfer) • Bone folder • Craft stick or old credit card for burnishing • Image on glossy stock or copy made on a toner-based copy machine (words, photo, clip art) • Water in a basin, tub, or bowl • Paper towels • *Hammerhead* Omni-Stick Clear gel adhesive

TIPS: You can transfer words or images from almost any paper surface, but glossy cardstock is the easiest to handle and gives the crispest image. • If you are printing a photo, use glossy cardstock rather than glossy photo paper for the transfer. Photo paper does not produce a good transfer. • The image will appear on the deco just as it appears on the original. There is no need to reverse the image before transferring. • Ensure images printed from a computer are completely dry before attempting the transfer. Pressure from burnishing the tape onto to printed image can smear wet or damp ink and degrade the image. • Words are easier to transfer than artwork with a solid background. Practice on words before advancing to solid-background images.

INSTRUCTIONS:
If you are printing the image from a computer, size the image to the desired dimensions. Print on glossy cardstock. • Cut the image from the sheet of paper, allowing a small border all around. Allow to dry completely. Place on the work surface image-side up. • Cut a piece of packing tape larger than the image to be transferred. Position the tape (sticky side down) over the printed image. Rub the tape with a bone folder to ensure a secure bond between the paper and tape with no air bubbles or creases. • Submerge the taped paper in clear tap water. Allow to soak for 1-2 minutes. • Begin rolling the paper away from the back using your fingertips, but not fingernails. *The goal is to remove as much of the paper as possible without disturbing the printed image.* You may leave as much or as little of the paper background as desired, just note that the more you are able to remove, the more transparent the finished transfer will be. • Blot the shiny side of the transfer with paper towels. Place it on a dry paper towel shiny side down to dry completely. • When the transfer is completely dry, trim to desired size and place on the deco in desired position. Sometimes enough of the tape's adhesive remains to provide a secure bond between the background and the transfer. If not, use a thin layer of clear gel medium or gel adhesive and weight in place until dry.

1. Apply tape to the image or words to be transferred. Burnish with a bone folder.

2. Submerge the taped paper in clear water. Soak for 1-2 minutes.

3. Peel off backing by rolling the paper away from the tape with your fingertips.